The Idea of an Essay: Volume 5
Two-tongued, Bach's Flute, and Homeschool

ISBN: 9781643165561
Cedarville University
Cedarville, Ohio 45314
Copyright 2018

Editorial Staff

The Composition Committee
    Dan Clark
    Mellissa Faulkner
    Andy Graff
    Isaac Mayeux
    Mary McCulley
    Cyndi Messer
    Michelle Wood

Editor
    Chelsea Clark

Design & Cover Art
    Chelsea Clark

Special thanks to the Cedarville University Department of English, Literature, and Modern Languages

The Department of English, Literature, and Modern Languages

Our Mission

Hello from Cedarville University, and thank you for your interest in the Department of English, Literature, and Modern Languages. Our programs produce men and women who communicate effectively and think deeply, cross-culturally, and creatively about the ideas that have shaped and continue to shape our world.

Our mission is to challenge students to go beyond expectations. Henry David Thoreau once wrote that we hit only what we aim at and thus ought to aim at something high. We agree — aim high. Who will write the definitive scholarly treatment of Don DeLillo's work? Who will share Christ by teaching English to migrant workers in west Michigan? Where is this generation's C.S. Lewis or Flannery O'Connor? At Cedarville University, we want our students to aspire to such heights.

Table of Contents

Letter to readers 1
Instructor Biographies 2
2018 Composition Contest Winners 9
    Two-tongued by Tamara Marques................... 10
    Analysis of the Paperman by Anna Lyons........... 14
    Bach's Flute Music by Sharri Hall.................... 19
    Homeschool Position by Johnna Willis............. 26
Narrative 37
    Big, Ugly by Isabelle Bendorf....................... 38
    Lit Narrative by Colin Dellaperute.................. 40
    On My Side by Tristan Galyon 45
    The Fine Art of Flying by Connor Tomlin 50
    Touching the Sky by Josiah Lansford................ 53
    Reminiscence of Home by Daniel Parschauer 58
    How Idiopathic Juvenile Osteoporosis Will Not
        Ruin Your Life… by Aubrey Podnar……... 63
    Blank Pages, Colorful Thoughts by Kimberly
        Powell………………………………………….. 68
    The Art of Crying by Presley-Peyton Shemelia.... 74
    Spiritual Training by Johnna Willis…………..... 77
Analysis 82
    Robots Guide to Ethical Marketing by
        Andrew Bidlen……………………………... 83

Catching Flowers off Choctaw Ridge by
    Abigail Brighton............................ 88
An Analysis of Luke Redd on Free Higher-
    Education by Sharri Hall ......…............. 95
Did Donald Stump the Nation? by Connor Tomlin
    Haynes…....................................…... 104
Paperman: A New Light to Lost Love by
    Lila Pattison.................................…... 110
To be Free or not to be Free that is the Question
    Kimberly Powell.................................…...119

Expository ………..….. 128
    Turbocharging by Tristan Galyon……….....…... 129
    Proprioceptive Neuromuscular Facilitation by
    Kelsey Howell………….........................…... 137
    A Homeschool Survey by Johnna Willis...........144

Argument ……….. 150
    The Proper Use of Proprioceptive Neuromuscular
    Facilitation by Kelsey Howell …………........151
    Pom Beanies are the Best by Brandon Ryan........163

Composition Student Learning Outcomes …............. 170
Grading System ……….....................................…...171
Plagiarism System ……….................................…...172
Writing Center ………..................................….. 173
Centennial Library ……….. 174

Dear Readers,

Welcome to Cedarville University. We are excited to have you in our composition classes. This anthology is meant to serve as a learning tool, and we will use it together over the course of this semester as we engage in the process of writing.

Cedarville University values writing. Regardless of your major, writing will be an intrinsic part of your education during your years at Cedarville, as it is a primary means of expressing clear, organized, critical thought. Perhaps more importantly, the writing you will do as part of your academic life will serve as practice for the various writing tasks each of you will complete as part of your chosen professions, as well as preparation for the writing you will do in your various communities, interpersonal relationships, and your daily devotions with God.

Cedarville University commits to preparing each of you to be successful writers by requiring a first-year composition course taught by a member of the English, Literature, and Modern Languages Department. As composition instructors, we recognize the excellent writing created in our classes, so we host an annual composition contest for students who completed the course during that year. The anthology you are about to read consists of the winners of that contest for the 2017-2018 academic year.

In the following pages, you will find models of university level writing, as well as examples of how to structure, organize, support, and document various genres of essays written for different purposes and with specific audiences in mind. We do not suggest these essays are perfect, as one of the most exciting aspects of writing is that it is a process that includes revision, so a text can always be improved upon or recreated as something different.

Each essay begins with an instructor's note that provides context for the essay and asks questions to prompt further ideas. The instructor's note is followed by a short biography of the student who wrote the essay to hopefully illustrate that, although these students are now published authors, they are not much different from you, the reader. You should find this encouraging. If these students can write successfully at the university level, then so can you.

Sincerely,
The Cedarville Composition Instructors

Instructor Biographies

Daniel Clark
Associate Professor of English

Professor Clark teaches courses in composition, advanced grammar, contemporary world literature, film, and the graphic novel. Along with Dr. Andrew Wiseman, Professor Clark developed Cedarville's foreign film series. He also serves as cosponsor of Alpha Kappa Delta, Cedarville's chapter of Sigma Tau Delta, the International English Honor Society. Before coming to Cedarville, he taught at the University of Maryland Asian Division in Okinawa, Japan. He also taught English as a Second Language (ESL) at the Okinawa Prefectural Language Center. Professor Clark has been at Cedarville since 1999.

Education and Credentials
- M.A. in English, University of Tennessee at Chattanooga
- B.A. in Secondary Education (with proficiencies in English and Bible), Tennessee Temple University

Interests
- Theology
- Film and contemporary world literature
- Japanese culture
- Comics, comix, graphic novels, manga, and bandes dessinées
- The Atlanta Braves (chop on!)

Contact Information
Email: clarkd@cedarville.edu

Melissa Faulkner
Associate Professor of English

Dr. Faulkner teaches Basic English, Composition, and Visual Rhetoric. She also serves as the coordinator for Writing Across the Curriculum. Her research interests include memoirs as retention and critical thinking tools, story analysis, and the organic connection between WAC programs and assessment. Dr. Faulkner has received multiple Excellence in Teaching awards, including one from the Southern Ohio Council of Higher Education.

Education and Credentials
- Ph.D., Miami University of Ohio
- M.A., Wright State University
- B.A., Wright State University

Contact Information
Email: mfaulkner@cedarville.edu

Andy Graff
Some kind of professor of English Professor

Andrew Graff joined the faculty of the Department of English, Literature, and Modern Languages in 2015. Andy's short fiction has appeared in Stolen Island and NPR's Three Minute Fiction. At Cedarville, he teaches Introductory and Advanced Fiction workshop, Introduction to Literature, English Composition, and a special topics course leading to the annual publication of The Cedarville Review.

Education and Credentials
- M.F.A. in Creative Writing with emphasis in Fiction, University of Iowa
- B.A. in English Literature, Lawrence University

Contact Information
Email: agraff@cedarville.edu

Isaac Mayeux
Assistant Professor of English

Isaac Mayeux has taught Composition at Cedarville since 2012. He also serves as the university's Director of Debate, Assistant Director of the Writing Center, and co-sponsor of Alpha Kappa Delta, Cedarville's chapter of Sigma Tau Delta, the International English Honor Society. Before coming to Cedarville, he taught Composition at the University of Dayton while studying for his M.A. He also taught English as a Second Language (ESL) in Seoul, South Korea for one year.

Education and Credentials
- M.A. in English and American Literature, University of Dayton
- B.A. in English, Cedarville University

Interests
- Graphic narrative (AKA comics)
- Animation
- Sport coats
- Christian poetics
- Complicated strategy board games
- Cultural criticism

Contact Information
Email: isaacjmayeux@cedarville.edu

Mary McCulley
Assistant professor of English

Mary McCulley joined the faculty of the Department of English, Literature, and Modern Languages in 2015. She grew up in Texas with four siblings and two godly, loving parents. The Lord saved me when I was around 8 years old and has called me to be actively involved in music and children's ministries since I was young.

Education and Credentials
- ABD in English, Texas Christian University
- M.A. in Rhetoric and Composition, Texas State University
- B.A. in English, Texas State University

Interests
- Piano
- Painting
- Reading
- Writing
- Hiking
- Decorating

Cyndi Messer

Associate Professor of English Professor Messer taught several years in secondary education before joining the faculty at Cedarville in 1998. She teaches general composition and literature courses as well as methods courses for future English teachers. She currently serves as the program coordinator for the Adolescent and Young Adult Language Arts (AYALA) majors and is a key contact for questions concerning the English education program. She also serves as faculty advisor for The Miracle, Cedarville's yearbook.

Education and Credentials
- M.A. in English, Wright State University
- B.A. in English Education, Cedarville College

Interests
- Favorite Places Visited: Paris, Puerto Vallarta, and San Francisco
- Hobbies: playing board games with family, exercising, reading, playing piano, gathering family and friends around a bonfire
- Favorite Authors: C.S. Lewis, Amy Tan, Thomas Hardy, John Steinbeck, Marilynne Robinson, Erik Lawson, and Shakespeare

Contact Information
Email: messerc@cedarville.edu

Michelle Wood
Associate Professor of English

Doctor Wood has been at Cedarville since 1995. Before coming to Cedarville, she taught English in Beijing, China. She has presented papers at national conferences, including the Conference on College Composition and Communication, the National Council of Teachers of English, the College English Association, and the Society for the Study of American Women Writers, speaking on topics such as Multigenre writing, Catharine Maria Sedgwick, Margaret Fuller, Alice Cary, and Amy Tan. Dr. Wood is a member of the Society for the Study of American Woman Writers and the Catharine Maria Sedgwick society.

Education and Credentials
- Ph.D. in Literature and Criticism, Indiana University of Pennsylvania
- M.A. in Composition and Rhetoric, Wright State University
- B.A. in English Education and Speech Education, Cedarville College

Interests
- Travel • Biking
- Archival research of women's life-writing
- College football

Contact Information
Email: woodm@cedarville.edu

2018 Composition Contest Winners

Best Narrative:
Tamara Marques

Best Analysis:
Anna Lyons

Best Expository:
Sharri Hall

Best Argument:
Johnna Willis

Tamara Marques—Best Narrative

Tamara Marques is a freshman computer science major from Portugal. In her writing, she draws inspiration from various authors she admires. She enjoys impromptu dance parties, hanging out with friends, and watching movies.

Two-tongued

I am bilingual.

Portuguese is my first language.

I first swam in it, completely immersed, when I was a baby. It was in Portuguese that I spat my first words. Portuguese is home. Its words paint pictures in my mind- black and white memories, dancing around my eyes like a slideshow. Portuguese is warm and breezy like a summer's night.

English is my second language.

I dipped into it when I was a toddler and later dived into it as I grew older. It was in English that I formed some of my first friendships. English is a key. It opens doors to new cultures. English is piquant and crisp, like an afternoon in October.

As a child, I struggled with having two languages fighting against each other, rattling in my brain. I would merge and blend them. I tampered with them- making them my own. I would use the words and phrases from each language that tasted better in my mouth. I loved the aromatic sweetness of Portuguese words mixed with the buttery gooeyness of English phrases. Separate they were nice to satisfy a specific craving for a feeling or sentiment, but together they tickled my emotional palate superbly. I took Portuguese words that did not exist in English and English words that did not exist in Portuguese. I would make sentences out of both of them. I had formed my own language. My sister and I still speak "Portlish" fluently - much to our mother's amusing despair.

However, I do despair (which I hardly find amusing) when both Portuguese and English fail to serve me as the correct communication devices. Sometimes I cannot seem to translate what I am thinking and seeing in my brain into real words. No matter how hard I try, I cannot avoid that dry feeling. The blankness my mouth experiences causes me to forget to articulate the exact words I wish to convey. The images in my mind and my feelings struggle to translate in fluent, coherent color. They fumble in a bleak black and grey. Both languages long to speak so badly that they block each other out. Their fight distracts me from what I am trying to say. This interior battle often causes my sister and I to struggle with speaking.

"Diz só em Inglês!" My sister suggests after I stutter and grunt frustratingly. "Just say it in English!"

"Eu não consigo, também me esqueci de dizer a palavra em Inglês!" I scoff at the two languages in my brain. Their common state is fight and conflict, but now they lay quiet and calm. So calm that they seem to be mocking me. I for some strange reason cannot utter that specific word through any of them about what I want to say. How dare they. I find their calm demeanor irritating. "I can't, I also forgot how to say it in English!"

The ends of my sister's mouth gradually turn up. Her eyes look up at the ceiling as she sighs. She knows my situation much too well. Both of our effervescent minds cause us to bubble laughter out of our mouths. Portuguese and English laughter foam out of our lips.

"Ai, rapariga só mesmo nós!" My sister would sing in between frothy giggles, "Only we would actually forget how to speak in two languages!"

I cannot ever forget to thank God that I have my sister to speak my language with. Many of my friends speak only one. I do have a select group of friends that have mastered Portlish, yet still we bilinguals mix the flavors of each language to our own liking. We always come up with different dialects.

I hardly ever mind that most of my friends only speak one language or the other. However, I do mind when my English speaking friends and my Portuguese speaking friends are in the same room together and I become the reluctant designated translator. My tongue turns into a slippery eel and my words sway awkwardly through my teeth. Fact: having to explain a joke in one language when it is only funny in the other can only contribute to awkward and forced laughs. Jokes are not usually polyglots by nature.

Languages come with their own culture. They live as words and phrases, yet they also mirror the feelings and thoughts of the people who speak them. I recommend imperatively using the correct idioms that correspond to the correct language. I would never say it was raining cats and dogs in Portuguese just like I would not say that it was raining pots and pans in English.

There can be so many layers of English and Portuguese I can speak. It depends on the audience. If I am with my teen friends, I speak in a more "broken" Portuguese with a dollop of Angolan slang and vocabulary. When I am at church and at home I speak a more traditional and proper "Lisbon" Portuguese accidentally spilled with a few grammatical mistakes that my mother often reprimands me of. She wishes I could speak more of the "correct" Portuguese. I do try to improve it, but it is a tough language to master. I am also fluent in other forms of English. I speak a more relaxed English with my bilingual friends - an English filled with slang to the brim. It tends to not be as posh or refined as the one I have to speak and write for my English assignments and emails for my classes here at Cedarville.

My mouth widens into a grateful smile whenever I remember the unbelievable opportunities I have had over the years, mostly because of God placing these two little guys in my brain. A group at my church which included my sister and me, translated Bible stories and sermons in Mozambique together with a mission's team from Michigan. I remember feeling overwhelmed about translating one language into the other, yet my sister helped me out with some of the grammar and idiom differences. My creamy Portuguese and crunchy English managed to work together. They helped the other English-minded people to communicate iridescent stories and lessons of the Bible to Portuguese-minded children in Mozambique. What a beautiful thing we accomplished. We made friends there due to our unique ability to speak in different languages.

I have developed strong attachments with people from their own different linguistic-cultured worlds. While the savory and crisp English bridged us together to explore each other's linguistic worlds, we managed to form a new one. A world where we all our languages purred in delight.

My languages still quarrel from time to time, sparking away as they try to move my mouth and have me think with them. Yet I can now control them a bit better and motion one to speak and the other to hush. However, I must be careful not to shun one so hard that it might flail and keep silent forever.

Knowing two languages was not always rosy. It came with its own prickly thorns. Nevertheless, the rose bloomed. My life as a bilingual is weird, yet colorful and fragrant with my own assembled words. My heart beams at this precious gift God has given me.

Anna Lyons—Best Analysis

Anna Lyons is a freshman nursing major from Claxton, Georgia. Outside of nursing, Anna plays the French horn in the Cedarville orchestra and is hoping to add a women's ministry minor to her time here at CU.

Analysis of the Paperman

John Kahrs, known for his animation work in *Tangled, Ratatouille, Incredibles,* and *Monsters Inc.*, purposefully directed the Disney short, *Paperman,* in a "stylized photorealism" to tell the story of a potential romance in which strangers have an abrupt initial encounter (Radish 2,7). Kahrs has hopped between Pixar and Disney animation productions (Radish 2). The techniques from each are shown through his stylistic choices to illustrate the story in an unfamiliar combination of varying techniques.

The *Paperman* received an Annie Award for best short film and an Oscar in 2013 (Oatley 2,7). Directors have discussed breaking the admired story down into a full length featured film (Oatley 12), but doing so would strip it of its intentional simplicity. Overall, audiences who first viewed *Paperman* as the featured short for *Wreck-It-Ralph* were awed and interested in the style and story work of the short (Oatley 10).

The concise but emotion catching short film tells the story of how a brief encounter flourishes into a relationship between two ordinary individuals on the streets of New York City. Most viewers perceive the text as a simple romance, but through the manipulation of color, sound, and physical structure, *Paperman* uses a love story to comment on the timeless issue of loneliness among people.

The absence of color and the antique aesthetic are at the forefront of Kahrs design for the *Paperman*. According to Jessica Mallinson's analysis, the short is a commentary that "love is timeless" for all of history (12). Kahrs uses black and white to illustrate a lonesomeness in the individuals' lives by lack of variety in color; though the city floods with people, no faces are familiar aside from their own reflections. When the woman is introduced, the audience's eyes are immediately drawn to her red lipstick as it stands alone in the color scheme. By having a sudden burst of color as in Figure 1, there is a moment of recognition beyond the paper man's typical quiet hustle of life. Red, in this particular short story, represents both romance and longing between the individuals. These specific details were intended to embody the longing to escape solitude. As the pair reunite at the train station, sunlight changes the hue of the final shot to represent a shift in emotions. The two are able to acknowledge a relationship and therefore step out of their state of loneliness put forth by their business driven lives.

    In addition to the plain color palette, there is only music, no commentary from characters. Just as there is a single accent of color, there is one moment in which the man's sigh is verbalized as he barely saves the lipstick marked paper from flying away. The instances that stand out represent a depth to the individuals that may not have been realized before they were highlighted. Kahrs spent a significant amount of time living a lonely life in New York City and comments on how he used to spend much time admiring the black and white images of the New York skyline (Macquirre 4). Through this and his time in crowded subways, he pondered on how many faces would go by, yet he still felt alone (Macquirre 4). By stripping the film of color and speech, Kahrs personifies a combination of his experiences and imaginations through the *Paperman*. Producer Kristina Reed shares that, "the cityscape serves as a visual metaphor for the lead character's isolation…" along with the lack of color (Macquirre 8).

Structure is a key strategy in relaying the underlying message of this short film. Both of the key characters in the story are tall and slender, resembling that of their background. The importance of body structure is most evident when the two are in the same shot. In Figure 2, the screen has all of the weight on one side which directs attention to the need of a balanced frame and likewise represents the paper man's lopsided social life. Figure 3 visually displays the way in which the woman counterbalances the paper man. The paper man also has a rectangular body with harsh sides yet his hair seems ruffled upon his soft edged face. This allows him to stand out slightly among his identical, sharp-edged co-workers in the paper company. The girl has much softer lines yet does have elements of rectangular definition such as her face and upper shoulders. This design promotes the idea that neither one identifies solely in a particular sect of society yet are embracing their individuality with which they both recognize in the other. The animation of the film is a first time combination of 2D hand drawn characters with 3D Computer-generated characteristics (Macquirre 3). The DNA of the short, similar to the characters, does not fit into one particular arena but is an experiment of distinctiveness.

    Paper is an important motif as well in this short film. When obscuring the clear-cut edges, the paper man causes strife in the office as he begins to fold flat, 8.5 by 11's into airplanes. As paper is suddenly seen by the paper man as a tool for reaching the woman, it represents that strange faces among the city can have more meaning--more possibilities--than what is initially assumed.

    Kahrs' short film is more than a romance clip; Paperman is an encouragement for the audience to reach beyond conforming to the norm. Though the story appears to be of a simple nature, Kahrs entwines intentional color, sound, and basic structure manipulations to represent difficulty in relationship formation as well as in the trials of loneliness. The characters' battle against loneliness is a timeless issue in culture and by addressing it, Kahrs is calling people to step out of their accepted dissatisfaction and to be in communion with one another.

Works Cited

Oatley, Chris. "The Making Of 'Paperman' and The Future Of DisneyAnimation." *ChrisOatleycom*, 26 Apr. 2016, http://chrisoatley.com/making-of-paperman/.

Macquarrie, Jim. "Disney's Paperman Is a Perfect Short Film." *Wired.com*, Conde Nast Digital, 12 Nov. 12ADAD, https://www.wired.com/2012/11/paperman/.

Mallinson, Jessica. "Textual Analysis: Paperman." *Jessica Mallinson A2 Media Blog*, 7 Sept. 2013, https://jessicamallinsona2.wordpress.com/2013/07/12/textual-analysis-paperman/.

Radish, Christina. "Director John Kahrs Talks PAPERMAN, How the Idea for the Short Came About, the Lack of Dialogue, Blending Traditional and CG Animation and More." *Collider*, 3 Nov. 2012, http://collider.com/john-kahrs-paperman-interview/.

Sharri Hall—Best Expository

Sharri K. Hall is a junior flute performance major from South Florida. She has been writing since she was young and hopes to pursue a career in the legal field. When she is not practicing the flute, she enjoys reading and planning obsessively.

Bach's Flute Music

Johann Sebastian Bach was a Baroque composer. He was an organ virtuoso, known for his keyboard compositions and contrapuntal works for instruments, keyboard, and voice. Bach established the context for music theory for several generations and is largely considered the pinnacle of Western tradition in music. Bach's music triumphed the end of the Baroque era, which music scholars credit for the development of tonality and tonal music.

Bach was a highly prolific composer. By his death in 1750, he had written several hundred compositions. Despite the scope of his collection, he composed fewer than ten of those pieces for the flute. Additionally, those few pieces are known to be exceedingly difficult to play on the modern concert flute in C. Some music scholars suggest that Bach's flute compositions are "unidiomatic and [show] no understanding of the qualities of the instrument." They argue that Bach neglected the tonalities and tessituras (range) of the instrument. As such, some scholars suggest that these pieces do not align with Bach's genius and were therefore composed by one of his students. Others suggest that since some of these pieces were definitely written by J.S. Bach, they suggest they may have been written for other instruments and later revised for flute. Other scholars, however, suggest that these difficulties exist because the pieces were written for a virtuoso, or especially talented performer beyond his/her years, that did not need to avoid certain difficulties. They may also suggest that these nuanced difficulties are better understood on a Baroque flute than on a modern flute. This essay does not seek to take a side; it aims to discuss and understand the difficulty and obscurity of Bach's writing for the transverse flute based on how Baroque style, the Baroque flute of Bach's time and his ultimate purposes in composing may have influenced his compositional choices.

The difficulty of Bach's flute compositions is better understood in the context of the style he was writing for. The Baroque era refers to the period of history between 1600 and 1750 typifying painting, architecture, and music as ornate, dramatic, and expressive. The Baroque style featured prominent bass and treble lines, and there was an uprising of melody and accompaniment style with basso continuo and figured bass (where the composer wrote a single bass line and left it to the performer to fill in the appropriate chords). The style features many diverse timbres in combination with the introduction of the concertato style (playing many instrumental voices against one another) and the concerto (a solo instrument set against an orchestra).

The Baroque era also derived "mean-tone" and "equal-tonality." These were tuning systems that offset the difficulty of tuning instruments of different timbres and preceded our modern system of tuning based on concert pitch a':440. This new system of tuning also initiated chordal harmonies (triads based upon three notes that resonate together in the scale) and dissonance (purposeful unpleasing sound). This system of tuning lead to the idea of tonality (music based around one key). The scalar systems of tonality allowed for chromaticism (using notes that do not belong in that key), counterpoint (point against point or note against note), and regular rhythmic patterns. Baroque music, particularly Bach's, highlighted the centrality of performance. It featured much ornamentation, alteration and improvisation, as well as cadenzas (extensions of pieces where the performer could highlight their virtuosic talent).

Bach undertook to highlight these characteristics in his compositions. He composed several sonatas (pieces for solo instrument and keyboard) for flute and keyboard that would combine the timbres of woodwind and plucked strings. More generally, he composed extensively in the fugal genres (settings of dense counterpoint where a subject is imitated through slight variations continually in all voices) and oratorios that featured full vocal chorus and a full orchestra. To target tonality, Bach only wrote in the keys that suited each instrument and only combined instruments that were well-suited for each other. For example, Bach rarely wrote for flute and violin because flutes were better suited to flat keys and violins were better suited to sharp keys. Most significantly, Bach was known for his impressive and excessive ornamentation. Turns and grace notes (notes added to leap into a heavy beat) are strewn throughout his music. Alteration was essentially required; it was understood amongst performers that it was appropriate to add ornamentation or even improvise as they saw fit. The flute severely limited Bach's compositional choices in that it could only play one note at a time. To counteract this limitation, Bach wrote virtuosic melodies and filled in the accompaniment with more contrapuntal styles. However, these pieces would be fundamentally more difficult to perform.

  The difficulties in Bach's compositions for flute are also better understood in the context of the instrument he was writing for. The Baroque flute is an enigma in that it is quite different from the modern concert flute in C and that it existed in several different forms. Three of these were particularly notable.

  The flûte d'amour was probably the most popular form of the instrument. It was a French flute with a lower range, having either a B or B-flat as its bottom pitch. It had a narrow bore which gave it an "atmospheric" sound and made it popular amongst Classical writers. The bass dessus de la flûte traversière was also a notable variant. It was a more refined version of the flûte d'amour and had a much wider bore. It existed in both French and English styles. The French style was wider at the foot with a large mouth hole and a "husky" sound, and the English style had the widest bore, but a beautiful sound. Lastly, there was the German/Dutch alto flute. The bore was considerably wider than that of the flûte d'amour but not as wide as the bass dessus. It had a conical bore and an undercut mouth hole that produced a sweet and expressive sound. There is debate about which specific flute Bach was writing for, but most settle on either the flûte d'amour or the German/Dutch alto flute.

The Baroque flute, unlike the modern flute which is tuned at concert pitch, was a transposing instrument (the music is notated at a pitch different from the pitch that actually sounds). These instruments would have transposed either a major or minor third above the concert pitch in the keyboard. The concert flute (haut dessus) was the first to tune at concert pitch, beginning in 1730.

It is important to consider that during this era, it was not usual to make distinctions about which flute a performer was expected to play on. The flutist would have looked at a score written in a certain key and immediately known whether he or she was meant to transpose. For example, a flutist would have known that a piece written in B major would have been transposed down a major third to be read in G major.

Bach certainly knew it was wise to avoid keys with several sharps or flats, because the instrument only had one key, but many tone holes (holes in the body of the instrument to cut off air flow and direct pitch) that required forked or crossed fingerings to achieve many sharps or flats. Composers and flutists were to avoid these forked fingerings because they produced a substantial difference in tone quality. They were often "weaker" in sound and would impair the strength of the performance. As such, we must expect that Bach's use of difficult keys were meant to be transposed into an easier key. Based on the keys in which they were written, the flute sonatas written between 1720 and 1730 were clearly written for the alto flute. If we follow these rules of transposition and apply them to the flute sonatas, we see that they have been written in keys such as G or D which feature only one and two sharps respectively.

Though Bach was a German composer, there was no predominantly German style of flute music. As such, it is understood that Bach wrote under the French theories and techniques for flute. Scholars believe that Bach may have taken his instruction for writing for the flute from L'Art de Préluder (1712) by Jacques Hotteterre. The manual gave detailed instructions on transposition and composition for the one-keyed flute.

Furthermore, due to imperfections in the making of the instruments, flutes often had ambiguous tonality. They would pitch at a slightly different note than others; if a flutist fingered a traditional D, a C-sharp may sound instead. As such, pieces for the flute were composed in ambiguous keys. Often, they were published in more than one key. The Hotteterre manual suggests several key pairings for flute and keyboard accompaniment. At the time, there existed a French clef that would make it possible for a keyboardist and flutist to read the same score and understand it in different keys. However, since no such clef existed in German music theory, Bach would have had to write separate scores for flute and keyboard to read in their own keys. This would have been tiresome and tedious. As such, German tradition sought, instead, to write the scores in the key necessary for the keyboardist and have the flutist transpose at sight.

Finally, the difficulty in Bach's compositions for flute are better understood in the context of his purposes in writing for the flute. Some scholars suggest that Bach may have composed to engage in flute literature. Though the instrument was quickly becoming as popular and as important as the violin, there were few compositions readily available. Bach may have been composing to add to the literature.

Bach may have also composed on commission. There is conjecture that Bach may have been writing for Frederick the Great, King of Prussia. Frederick had been creating a "music lab" where he was experimenting with many different types of instruments and trying to make improvements upon them. Frederick and Johann Quantz had been trying to make a concert flute in C. This flute would have been innovative, but wildly different from the traditional Baroque flute. Addington suggests that Bach, ever the conservative, may have composed these pieces to fit only with a bass dessus flute to convince the pair to forget their ties to this new concert flute. History suggests Bach may have been successful because the Quantz flute never became a popular model and was never used as a model for newer flutes.

Studying the difficulties in Bach's compositions suggests that some of his works may have been commissioned by talented flutists and not amateurs; they may have been professionals who were constantly working on honing their talent. As such, Bach would have had the opportunity to write much more complex, dexterous, and virtuosic pieces. Accordingly, some scholars argue that Bach paid so much attention and detail to the flute because he was particularly fond of it. As such, he spent more time making these pieces more difficult to play.

Bach's compositions for flute are generally understood as being particularly difficult compositions. Some scholars even suggest they were not composed by him or that they were not initially composed for the flute, but revised from compositions for other instruments. It is easier to understand the difficulty of Bach's compositions in the context of the style they were being written in, the inherent complexities of the Baroque flute, and Bach's purposes in composing for flute. With that in mind, Bach's flute compositions can be understood more clearly and flutists can have a more informed opinion about the authenticity of the authorship.

Bibliography

Addington, Christopher. "The Bach Flute." The Musical Quarterly 71, no. 3 (1985): 264–80. ttp://www.jstor.org/stable/948156.

Ambrose, Jane. "The Bach Flute Sonatas: Recent Research and a Performer's Observations." Bach 11, no. 3 (1980): 32-45. http://www.jstor.org/stable/41640107.

Burkholder, J. Peter, Donald Jay Grout, and Claude V. Palisca. A History of Western Music. 9th ed. Edited by Maribeth Payne. New York: W.W. Norton & Company, 2014.

Charles Sanford Terry. Bach's Orchestra. London: Oxford University Press, 1961.

David, Hans T. and Arthur Mendel, eds. The Bach Reader: A Life of Johann Sebastian Bach in Letters and Documents. New York: W.W. Norton, 1972.

Jeremy Montagu. The World of Baroque and Classical Musical Instruments. New York: The Overlook Press, 1979.

Marshall, Robert L. "J. S. Bach's Compositions for Solo Flute: A Reconsideration of Their Authenticity and Chronology." Journal of the American Musicological Society 32, no. 3 (1979): 463-98. doi:10.2307/831251.

Powell, Ardal, and David Lasocki. "Bach and the Flute: The Players, the Instruments, the Music." Early Music 23, no. 1 (1995): 9–29. http://www.jstor.org/stable/3137801

Johnna Willis—Best Argument

Johnna Willis is a sophomore early childhood education major from Huntington, West Virginia. From a young age she has been interested in the development of the next generation's mind. Since then she has offered children's piano lessons and served at her state church camp.

Homeschool Position

Homeschooling has been available to families for centuries, but it has recently become prevalent around the United States, reaching 1.77 million children in 2011 (*Homeschool Statistics*, 2016). This large number of children represent many families and homes. In most households, the parents decide if they desire to homeschool their children or if they want to send their children to a public or private school. A parent's freedom to homeschool their children is a considerable option in America today. Homeschooling has many variations across the country, from methods to resources to requirements, but throughout the options, the choice to educate at home is a good opportunity for children.

One aspect of homeschooling that makes it desirable for many families is that homeschooling is different for every child. Customizing curriculum is an option for most families who homeschool; therefore, each child receives a unique education that can usually caters to their needs. Kathleen Berchelmann, MD, quit working in the medical field to stay home with her children. She wrote in Children's MD's section *Mom Docs*, "Our kids are excelling academically as homeschoolers. Homeschooling allows us to enrich our children's strengths and supplement their weaknesses. The kids' education moves as fast or as slow as required for that particular subject area. They are not pigeon-holed and tracked as gifted, average, or special needs" (Berchelmann, 2015). Families customize their curriculum because children each work in a different way. Children in the homeschool setting occasionally study at desks at home, but there might be a school table where multiple children work or a computer desk where they sit and work on their materials and lessons for the day. This difference in environment compared to public or private schools is beneficial for most students, for the setting provides fewer distractions. It is especially helpful for students with special needs. For example, children with autism can have accommodations made at home that students cannot find in a classroom. Many homes where special needs children live already have the accommodations built in, therefore the child can learn without frustrations and with a familiar setup. Children with Attention Deficit/Hyperactivity Disorder (ADHD) can also benefit from home education because the environment can change in order to create a learning setting most productive for their needs. Parents and other educators can help with confidence at home, for there are no children for the students to compare themselves to and there are no bullies.

  The way in which children work often corresponds with the way they best think. Psychologist Howard Gardner's multiple intelligence theory states each mind has various strengths and weaknesses (Rathus, 2014). Focusing material to specific strengths, such as musical learners learning English rules through song, tends to help children learn more efficiently. When parents choose to homeschool, they choose to take education into their own hands which can adapt materials and subjects to reach their child's needs and strengths within their brain functioning and capacity.

  Because of accommodations such as creating the ideal curriculum, statistics show homeschooling works well for families nationwide. According to the U.S. Department of Education, 1.77 million children registered as homeschooled in 2011 (Homeschool Statistics, 2016). This number has dramatically increased in the past few decades. Author and educator Joseph Murphy researched the reasons behind the decision parents make to keep their children at home rather than send them to a public or private school. In his studies, he noted families choose to homeschool for various reasons, but the top contributing factors include academics, school social issues, religion, and family (2014).

Lisa Rivero presents a list of reasons why families choose to homeschool throughout the United States in her book The Homeschooling Option: How to Decide When It's Right for Your Family. Her reasons include the flexibility of schedule, the safety of the child, the encouragement of family bonding, and the specificity for each student (2008).

    Rivero's first point in her argument states, "Homeschooling works because it allows children to work at their own pace" (2008). Here, not only can parents establish a curriculum that works best with their child's brain functioning, but parents can establish a schedule that provides the optimal timing for children to get their best work completed. Bells do not ring and class periods do not change within the home. Each child stands alone and therefore can usually work longer on harder subjects, depending on the parents' preference. Homeschooling also does not have a start date and end date for Summer or Christmas breaks, so if a student needs more time on a subject in October, they can take time to work on that concept. Snow days do not apply either, which allows parents to choose a break day in other seasons if they need a day off. The schedule throughout the day varies, so children can sleep in and stay up late, if that is what works best for them and their parents. Seton Home Study School shares with its families "Science and history could be done on weekends or in the evenings with Dad or grandparents if more time is needed during the week for the other subjects" (Homeschool Success Through a Flexible Schedule, 2013). The parents choose the arrangements made for their children, not a principal or government. This angle works well with families who have children with learning disabilities. Oftentimes, children with needs such as dyslexia take a longer time to learn or need special teaching treatment. Homeschooling is a valid option for these children for they can receive this special alternative with little inconvenience to the instructor and with no worry of peer problems.

  This leads to the second point made by Rivero. She continues with the statement, "Homeschooling works because it provides a safe learning environment." (2008) The highest single response given in the U.S. Department of Education's survey asking why families chose to homeschool was parents' concern about the environment of the school the children would attend (Reasons Parents Homeschool, 2014).
In the home, the child normally feels comfortable. There are no class threats in the home. Children do not need a security guard walking the hallways or inspectors checking on lockers for safety measures. Parents staying home with children do not need special arrangements to take their students on a field trip in a bus or other school transportation. Parents and close friends orchestrate any trips for education which allows the families access to all information and confirmation of safety for their child. Because of these comforting measures, parents feel better about their child's well-being and the child is not distracted in what is supposed to be a learning setting. Not only can a parent ensure the safety by monitoring their child's environment physically, but the concern of peer pressure and bullying can also be closely watched. Sometimes school systems have a variety of children attending, and parents never know what certain children will say or do in front of their child. For protective purposes, a homeschooling family can stay actively involved in the child's environment and keep an eye on a child's friends and influences.

  The topic of influences leads to the common argument against homeschooling: if children stay at home they will not make any friends or get any kind of social interaction. This is, as a whole, untrue. The belief that no classmates means no friends usually is a false assumption. Many homeschoolers throughout the country have friends from organizations such as girl scouts, activities such as local sports leagues, and communities such as church families.

Another large resource for homeschooled children to receive socialization is through cooperation groups, or "co-ops," where several homeschool families from a region get together regularly for activities such as physical education classes, tutoring, field trips, and fun days off. Cooperation groups typically can be found around the country, but not in every area. This not only helps the children make friends from similar backgrounds, but it gives the parents a chance to get out of the house and spend time with other adults. "Co-ops" are often family-based with activities for all ages, but they are still an option for homeschooling families with only one child.

    For the families who choose to educate more than one child at home, Rivero continues to make the third claim, "Homeschooling works because it strengthens and nurtures families" (2008). When the When the children are younger, they typically develop a strong bond with their parents due to the necessity to be with them frequently. If there are multiple children, they separate during the school day to go to their various classes. Both of these separations do not occur in homeschooling. Many homeschool families work on classes together, go on field trips together, and eat meals together. Spending time together and making joint memories builds relationships between family members. Stefani, a homeschooling mother and blogger, talks about this older-younger sibling bond in her article *Learning is Better Together: Fostering Strong Sibling Relationships*. Her experience is expressed, "When we are working together to help our youngest learn something new, my older boys are learning that childhood is precious, short and worth cherishing. They are learning that having a younger person around is a real gift!" Testimonies such as this occur frequently among families who choose to keep their children home.

    This story from Stefani seems heartwarming and encouraging, but not every family gets these results when they attempt to homeschool. Some parent-child relationships undergo stress when they spend large amounts of time together. Children have the duel mindset of a parent and a teacher, and for smaller children this may become confusing. The parents also could feel bad about the grades they must give their children which creates tension between parent and child.

The parents and the children both sacrifice when they stay at home, but families who homeschool come to the decision that the better education is worth it. Rivero's final point says, "Homeschooling works because all children's needs are worthy of special attention" (2008). Each child is special and learns uniquely. A classroom teacher teaches to a classroom, that is all he or she is expected to do with his or her classroom. This method, however, does not reach each child's needs. Select teachers can assist students who struggle or excel, but the majority of the time the teacher must teach to the children as a whole. With the homeschooling method parents or home educators can cater the material particularly for that specific child. Just like the argument of reaching the child's specific intelligences (such as those Gardner theorized) and the pacing argument made by Rivero previously, the specificity of education program proves to be one of the more important reasons why families choose to homeschool.

Homeschooling may not be the best option, depending on the child and family situation. Specificity is helpful in a child's education, but some children require the social and discipline aspects of attending a school with classmates and teachers. Rivero counters her own argument of the benefits of homeschooling with, "All children- homeschooled or not- can lack self-discipline or parental guidance and example. If a child ceases to show interest in or engagement with life, parents would be wise to look carefully at what might need to be changed in the child's environment, habits of thought, self-concept, or family dynamics" (2008). Different children require different learning environments; therefore, they may need to be in a school setting. Each child has his or her own needs that can be met by either a home-based education or a private or public school education. This involves the parents' knowledge of the child's performance and a discussion between parent and child. It could be great for a specific child to stay home rather than attend a nearby school; it also may be a wonderful decision for the mother or father who would enjoy teaching. Unfortunately, however, if that child is strong-willed and does not want to do his or her schoolwork and the parents cannot find him or her new motivation, the best option may be to send the child to a new school setting that might encourage him or her to learn and take education seriously. Therefore, the needs presented by the student may be different than what the student wants, which requires special decision making by the parents and the schools.

Hard decisions such as deciding for or against a child's will are just one aspect of the struggle of homeschooling. As great as it may sound at times, homeschooling can prove difficult for many families. The main problem in the transition to homeschool typically resides with the parents. Rivero says, "When child-directed learning works well, it can require even more parental involvement, time, guidance, and skills than more traditional homeschooling approaches." (2008) Parents who choose to homeschool accept a full-time and important job of orchestrating their child's education.

Most families face challenges when considering staying home to educate their children or hiring someone to come teach. When families homeschool, usually the mother stays home to assist in the education rather than work a full-time job. This results in a decrease in the family's income, even if the mother switched to a part-time job or hired a tutor to homeschool the children. Unfortunately, due to these circumstances, many families' only option financially is to send their children to a public school.

Worries about income can weigh in greatly on a family's decision to homeschool, but other families worry about the politics involved in the reports to the state about their children's education. The majority of states in the United States have regulations regarding how they keep up with children who are not in the public-school system. Depending on where the family is located, the state laws may post an issue in the homeschooling field. The Home School Legal Defense Association (HSLDA) mapped out the states in which homeschooling is easiest and most difficult. Regulations vary by region. High regulation states (5 states, all in New England) require parents to turn in to the state the student's test scores, teacher certification, house tests, and get their curriculum approved by the state (Davis, 2013). Moderate level regulation (19 states nationwide, including Hawaii) requires turning in to the state the student's test scores (Davis, 2013). Low regulation states (15 states, mostly in the south and the west) just require parents to inform the state that their child will no longer attend a public school (Davis, 2013). Some states (11 states nationwide, including Alaska) have no regulations (Davis, 2013). These demographics greatly contribute to the way in which parents teach and view home education.

  The state may control an aspect of homeschooling, but, as a whole, the family environment contributes the most to whether or not the homeschool method is successful. As stated previously, sometimes the family environment changes when parents keep their child or children home. Spending a majority of their time at home together might be great for the strength of the family, but it might create problems that might create stresses within the home. Parents have been known to show frustration in teaching subjects they are not qualified to teach and in turn their attitude effect the child's behavior and attitude toward learning. Other parents get tired of spending all day with their kids rather than with other adults. The decision to homeschool does not only involve the child's needs and preferences, but the parents'.

  Overall, homeschooling is a team effort between parents, siblings, school systems, children, and the state's regulations. Homeschooling is a fantastic option for many families nationwide. The majority of parents who homeschool chose that route because of the flexibility in curriculum and schedule, the environment it creates, and the way the child performs in another school setting. However, not every family can or should homeschool. Difficulties at home create a negative environment in which children can learn, financial resources do not always allow a parent or tutor to teach the children privately, the children may thrive in their schools, and state requirements could provide issues in the home educational system. Therefore, although homeschooling is a wonderful and considerable freedom allowed in America that thousands of families take advantage of, it is not the preferable option for every family.

References

Berchelmann, K., MD. (2013, March 25). 18 Reasons Why Doctors And Lawyers Homeschool Their Children. Retrieved November 20, 2016, from http://childrensmd.org/uncategorized/why-doctors-and-lawyers-homeschool-their-children-18-reasons-why-we-have-joined-americas-fastest-growing-educational-trend/

Davis, T. (2013, September). *The Most Home-School-Friendly States in the US (and the least)*. She Knows. Retrieved October 15, 2016, from http://www.sheknows.com/parenting/articles/1018417/which-states-are-best-for-homeschooling

Homeschool Statistics. (2016). Retrieved October 14, 2016, from https://www.time4learning.com/homeschool/homeschoolstatistics.shtml

Homeschool Success through a Flexible Schedule. (2013, October 7). Retrieved November 17, 2016, from http://www.setonhome.org/4183/homeschool-success-through-a-flexible-schedule/

Murphy, J. (2014). *Homeschooling in America: Capturing and Assessing the Movement*. New York, NY: SkyHorse

Rathus, S. A. (2014). *Childhood & Adolescence: Voyages in Development* (5th ed.). Belmont, CA: Wadsworth Cengage Learning.

Reasons Parents Homeschool. (2014). Retrieved November 20, 2016, from http://www.responsiblehomeschooling.org/homeschooling-101/reasons-parents-homeschool/

Rivero, L. (2008). *The Homeschooling Option: How to Decide When It's Right for Your Family*. New York, NY: Palgrave Macmillan.

S. (2011, June 1). *Learning Is Better Together: Fostering Strong Sibling Relationships*. Retrieved November 15, 2016, from http://simplehomeschool.net/author/stefani/

Statistics About Nonpublic Education in the United States. (2015, June 9). Retrieved October 16, 2016, from http://www2.ed.gov/about/offices/list/oii/nonpublic/statistics.html

Narrative

Isabelle Bendorf
Colin Dellaperute
Tristan Galyon
Connor Tomlin Haynes
Josiah Lansford
Daniel Parschauer
Aubrey Podnar
Kimberly Powell
Presley-Peyton Shemelia
Johnna Willis

Isabelle Bendorf

Isabelle Bendorf is a sophomore psychology major from Pennsylvania. She has a particular proclivity for procrastination and loves creative writing, listening to music, and spending time with friends.

Big, Ugly

    Tired eyes squint into the dark wardrobe as my fingers lazily divide each hanger. I pass over each familiar fabric as I decide, *No, this is not who I will be today.* Soon I find the one. The thick collar slides off the curved plastic. The hangers swing back and forth, nervously tapping together. Worn threads graze my face and settle heavily on my shoulders.

    I turn to the mirror to give myself a once-over. *Good enough.* This sweater dragged itself out of the dark side of the 90s: my grandmother's dresser. It looks like the embodiment of the morning after a hard night of drinking. The indigo threads emphasize the fatigue that lies beneath my eyes. The wrists billow and hang well past my fingers. Sure enough, I reacquaint myself with this person. It's been a few weeks since we've seen each other so we share a tentative embrace, still unsure of whether we will be friends today.

    Most onlookers might assume that I am careless or apathetic or lazy; at least, that's what I think they might assume. However, I'd hope they would see me as relaxed or comfortable with who I am, even if just for the moment. *Even if I don't know exactly who I am.* There's a type of security in a good sweater. I could be wearing a shirt underneath that says, in big bold letters, "NEUROTIC," and no one would have any idea. I can still hide who I am in plain sight. My comfort lies in my concealment.

Maybe I should change. I can wear this later when I'm alone. This disguise is easier to overlook when I'm alone. My own judgements don't seem quite as harsh when they are not accompanied by the eyes of strangers. Besides, it pools at the waist and wrists, making it difficult to use my hands; almost like a cozy cilice. It doesn't offer me much in terms of warmth; holes have started to form over the years. They have become the perfect windows into my failing façade for anyone who looks too close.

My fear jitters underneath my skin and lingers in my chest. I am terrified of the time that those dreaded words will finally achieve their vice-like grip on my eardrums. "What's wrong?" My heart throbs just thinking about it. I can see myself crumbling beneath the weight of the question. I can see the dust falling through those worn holes.

I'll deal with the biting wind and the way it passes through the stitches. I'll deal with the oversized nature of it because it's my favorite aspect. I'll deal with the judgmental second-glances that aren't really there.

I know I shouldn't pay mind to my fears. *No one looks as closely at the frays and flaws than I do.* It's not all that terrible when I see others in the same predicament as myself. Maybe they're relaxed. Maybe they're on the brink of a mental breakdown. But you'd never know because a sweater is the perfect mask.

Looking in the mirror, I still can't fool myself. I still see the person that is terrified to make too much noise in a crowded room, whose face burns bright red when speaking in front of a class, who fears that others will see the same anxious person that I see when looking in a mirror. Regardless, I'll be this person today and hide who I really am. *But then again, maybe not.*

Colin Dellaperute

Colin Dellaperute is a sophomore communications major from South Jersey. He likes writing for fun in his spare time. Some of his other hobbies include playing soccer, playing guitar, and eating food.

Lit Narrative

Literacy has shaped my life in more ways than I can imagine. *Just kidding,*
I only said that so I could get my cliché saying out of the way.

  Honestly, literacy has not "shaped my life" in any significant way, but I can probably stretch some stuff from my life's experience, take some other stuff out of context, put it all together, and punch out around 800-1200 words. Sound good? Ok good, let's get to work.

  I grew up in a family that loves to read. My dad is a pastor, so he reads books with massively obnoxious titles like *The Ancient Church's Theology on Predestination, Hermeneutics, and Another Really Big Word vol. 17* just for the fun of it. My mom is into those Francine River-love-flower-sappy-type books, I think. My two youngest brothers are at that beginner-to-amateur reading stage where they will either read *Lord of the Rings*-type books or *Diary of a Wimpy Kid*-type books. My other brother, who is a year younger than me, likes to "challenge himself" (show off) and read books that look like they should be illegal for the amount of paper they use. He recently got done with *The Count of Monte Christo,* a book that would probably make me keel over and die. That, my friends, brings me to the main point of this paragraph. I know very well that this paper is a literacy paper and will ultimately end up in the hands of my composition professor, so I would like to warn you that what I am about to write will most likely make you think that I am a horrible person who likes to go around kicking puppies and popping children's balloons. I really hope that it does not give you that impression.

Here it is—*I am not a big reader.*

Surprise! If you couldn't already tell from my immature writing style and lack of big word usage.

I don't enjoy reading very much and it is a true struggle for me to power my way through a book. Trust me, I really wish I enjoyed reading, but it is something I have to force myself to do. I cannot merely sit down, relax, and enjoy a good book like normal people. Instead, I need to get a notebook, some highlighters, and a pen and take notes on the material in order for me to focus and comprehend what I am reading. It is a brutal process, and is the main reason why I would much rather do almost any other type of activity other then read, unfortunately.

     I actually kind of wish that I was a good reader. I know for a fact that I could be a great reader if I were to really work at it, but… well… let me put it this way; reading is kind of like being an alcoholic.

Bear with me you Baptists, this metaphor has a point.

There are five stages for each category.

The first stage in this twisted metaphor is the "*gag stage*". Both the drinker and the reader cannot stand their respective items and gag at the sight or smell of them. Next, we have the "bearable but still kind of nasty" phase. The items of the respective categories are still not appealing to the corresponding audiences, but they know that if they do them for long enough, it will lead them to phase three. Phase three is "occasionally on special occasions." Both the reader and beer-guzzler are slowly being acclimated to their categorical items, but still have some restraint and therefore only indulge every-so-often. Soon, "every-so-often" becomes not often enough, and their long journey (to either alcoholism or reading) ends. Now, the metaphor obviously has some holes in it. Reading won't cause your liver to fail or cause you to make stupid choices, *unless you are reading The Twilight Saga,* but the point I am trying to make is that it would take a lot of pain, sorrow, and weeping to change a person who does not like to read into an avid reader.

    Now, the overarching statement that I made in the above paragraphs was basically, "I am not a big reader and I don't enjoy it very much." I did not say that I hate reading or that I think reading is not valuable.

I do not hate reading; I am just not into it.

Although it is not a pastime that I generally love, I do understand the need for a regular amount of reading. There have been multiple studies done that show how reading can improve brain connectivity and function, and how it most likely improves one's overall intelligence. It is something that everyone *should* do, whether they enjoy doing it or not.

    My parents knew very well the importance of reading and have always encouraged me to read, even when I didn't like it. I vaguely remember my parents reading different books to me when I was young. One memory that stands out from all of the other book-related-emotional-flashback-stuff is when my mom used to read me this book before bed called *Love You Forever.*
I know, I know, it's super cheesy. But I was like five years old people!
It has been a while since I've picked up that book and read it, *mainly because I didn't want to be seen in public reading a book called Love You Forever,*

but I remember the story line very well. It told the story of a boy and his mom. Through every stage of life—through the tough stage of toddler-hood, through the know-it-all tween stage, through the rebellious teenager stage, through the struggles of adulthood—the mother always said these words to her son: "I'll love you forever, I'll like you for always, as long as I'm living, my baby you'll be." Every time my mom finished reading me that book, she would then say those words to me. Since I was only five years old, I didn't really pay much attention to those words; I was focused more on the picture of the toddler on the front cover pulling all of the toilet paper off of the rack. I thought that it was the greatest thing ever. But those words really did not mean much to me then.

A short time ago, I overheard my mom reading that same book to my youngest brother. Afterword, she said those same words to him; "I'll love you forever, I'll like you for always, as long as I'm living, my baby you'll be." As she said those words, my mind was taken back to when she read that same book to me. It kind of gave me this weird feeling that I really don't like to show. Since I am a man, I do the typical "manly" thing and try not to show very much emotion at all, let alone emotion of sadness. But it was at that moment, when I heard those words, I was overcome with this mixture of sadness and regret, or at least I think that was it. I was now almost at this adulthood stage of life, and have made so many mistakes and said so many regretful things towards both of my parents. Those words brought back so many unpleasant memories of me being a jerk to my mother in my teenage years. It reminded me of all of the times when I yelled at my dad for "embarrassing" me in front of my friends at school. It reminded me of all of the talking back, arguing, and bad attitudes that I constantly threw at them.

Yet, they still loved me.
They still did things for me to show their love for me.
They still cooked for me.
They still paid for my schooling.
They still bought me presents at Christmas.
They were always be there if I was struggling with something.
They still loved me in spite of how badly I treated them. That children's book that my mother read to me all those years ago means more to me now than it ever did in my life. It is a reminder that I really don't know how much longer I will have with my parents. I could have fifty more years. I could have a week. Every time I see that book, I am reminded of my parent's love for me and how I need to cherish every second I have left with them.

    As I begin to subside this whirlwind (or train-wreck) of a paper, I'm going to be honest with you all and confess that I have no idea how to end it. I don't want to just leave it like this, because the previous sentence in the last paragraph would leave you kind of sad, and I wouldn't want that. I also don't want to go ahead and end with some famous quote either because it would be really typical and predictable of papers like this. I guess what I will do is just keep writing this paragraph and see what my brain comes up with. Or maybe I'll try to come up with a clever ending and some special way to apply this to your life. Or maybe I'll make a funny joke. Or I'll… I don't know, writing is so hard, I really need to improve. I guess I should read more.

Tristan Galyon

Tristan Galyon is a sophomore majoring in mechanical engineering from Chicago. He enjoys reading and writing, as they require a different sort of thinking than engineering problem sets.

On My Side

My mother went to exactly one parent-teacher conference throughout the entirety of my education. It was my sixth grade year; every year before and after that, the conferences didn't fit into her busy schedule. She worked an incredible amount, and traveled very often for her job. Repeatedly for months on end, she'd fly out of our home airport, Chicago-O'Hare, early Monday morning, returning home late Friday night or in the predawn Saturday, only to do it all over again in 48 hours. Despite her busyness, she went to great lengths to ensure that I was doing what I needed to do to learn. Having received a third-world education herself, she was a huge proponent of the many opportunities schooling provided. Since we rarely saw each other in person during the week, she would call me on our home phone every night; one of her first questions was invariably, "What did you learn at school today?" She was as involved as she could be, without being an overbearing omnipresent PTA mom, and I respect her for it to this day. It never worried me that my mother could never come to parent-teacher conferences, nor do I think that my education was hindered in any way. By all realistic measure, she didn't need to meet with my teachers; she was a teacher's dream parent in terms of caring about their child's education.

In sixth grade, it worked out that she could finally come to a conference of mine. I was quite excited, given that my mother was going to see my school and meet the teachers that I had been working so hard for all year. She'd left work early that day, and had called me earlier to let me know at what time she would she would be home. She knew we'd be cutting it close as far as making it to school before conferences ended; our hope was for her to meet and talk to as many of my teachers as possible in the limited time she'd been able to allot at the end of the conference schedule. The plan was the usual one when we were on a tight schedule: she'd call me from the car when she got into our neighborhood, and I'd lock up the house and be waiting for her when she pulled in the driveway. When the white Nissan arrived, I gave the house's back door one last shake to make sure it was locked, and I climbed into the car.

We arrived at the school and I guided my mother to my classrooms and teachers. I was excited to introduce her to the place where I spent so much of my time. We went to my math course, where Mrs. Thompson spoke highly of me; to my social studies teacher, Mr. Murphy, who commented on my diligent work; and finally to my English classroom, taught by Mrs. Hildy. Mrs. Hildy and I had all the groundwork laid for a good teacher-student relationship; I was a voracious reader who loved to write, and she taught the subject that dealt with those things. I performed well in her class, and had no reason to dislike her. I was prepared for the night's final parent-teacher conference to go as well as the others, if not better.

Hildy's classroom had been rearranged slightly for conferences, with a small round table placed near the front, surrounded by three chairs. My mother and I sat close together, facing my instructor. The two women, opposite each other, were strikingly different pictures of the female professional. To my left was my mother, a no-nonsense woman who commanded respect in her dark business suit and conservative jewelry. My teacher, by contrast, sat across from her in a gray hooded sweatshirt with the school logo on the front, an outfit piece thoroughly supplemented by jeans and gym shoes. My mom's short salt-and-pepper hair betrayed her age, while the younger woman's hair was longer and would remain as it was for many years before she considered dyeing it. Even their hands were different as they passed papers between each other. My mother wore only one ring other than those from her engagement and wedding, and her hands looked slightly weathered, typical for her age. Hildy's hands were more youthful, and a finger was rare without a ring on its adjacent at the minimum. She smelled flowery, airy, and very young. My mother, by contrast, wore a perfume that was less sticky, a heavier, more professional scent. It wasn't overpowering, with an androgynous musk as opposed to my teacher's almost sickly sweetness. I paid minimal attention to the meeting itself; I had little reason to, given my expectations. Mrs. Hildy told my mother about her class, about what papers we'd written throughout the year, and what my grades had been. She gave my mother copies of grade reports, and generally conducted the meeting as if I wasn't there. Other teachers had made a limited effort to involve me, but Hildy made no attempt beyond acknowledgement. That was fine; the conference was for my mother, not for me. It wasn't until the meeting began to come to an end that my teacher brought up what had been on her mind throughout her time with me, saying,

"Your son is a good student, as we discussed." She paused, searching for a tactful statement through which she could make her point. "But I'm worried that he isn't making friends." Her eyes flicked to me, as if she expected some sort of response. I gave her none, not because I was denying emotion on any sort of principle, but because her statement surprised me.

My mother and I had the same objection, but only one of us had the power to address the issue via inquiry. "What makes you say that? My son talks about his friends all the time."

"I misspoke. I more meant that he doesn't seem to do what everyone else does when they have free time in class. Every chance he gets, he's pulling out a book." What she said was absolutely true – at every opportunity, I'd take out a book I'd brought with me from home or checked out from the library, and I'd read. Even if the break was only a few minutes, I would read my books. I simply loved to read, and I took every opportunity to do what I loved. Though my book reading was astonishingly consistent, I was not one to separate myself from a group or avoid others. I would not hesitate to turn around and chat with other students, nor was I afraid of public speaking. I knew I wasn't antisocial, and I was taken aback when my teacher seemed to say otherwise. I was astonished further still that she pointed to books as being the root cause of my apparent problem. I could recall schools stressing the importance of reading ever since the skill was first taught, and my passion for books had been praised at every level. Yet at that moment, I sat across from someone, an educator, who was telling my mother that I should read *less*.

My mother had a reaction only the best could have asked for: she cracked a smile and exhaled that sharp rush of air of someone hearing something that bordered on humor. To her, even the implication that a student could read too much was ridiculous. She had consistently encouraged my reading from the beginning, and she continued to do so in that moment. She gathered her things and said to my English teacher, "I'm not going to tell my son to stop reading." There was no anger in her tone, no malice. It was simple fact; amusement still lingered on her face. She thanked my teacher for her time, and we left the classroom. The black metal door shutting behind us with a dull thud was the only sound to accompany our footsteps as we walked down the hallway back towards the front of the building. Nothing was different; I struggled to keep up with my mother's fast pace, but that was usual. I didn't need or want her to change anything because I knew in that moment that what my mother had done was right, at least on a personal level. In that moment, my mother had gone to bat for me. She defended what she saw as a positive thing, the pursuit of knowledge. She continued to emphasize the importance of reading books for years, and always encouraged me to learn and discover things through literature. At the time of my sixth grade parent-teacher conference, I was grateful was grateful that my mother supported me. As time passed, that gratefulness came to be in conjunction with a great respect. She made many personal sacrifices for my sake, but one compromise she would not entertain would be one that inhibited my learning. She wanted what was best for me, and she was always on my side.

Connor Tomlin Haynes

Connor is a sophomore nursing major from Indianapolis. She enjoys participating in musical theatre productions and writing blogs for various companies.

The Fine Art of Flying

I have seen plenty of others perform these simple steps before; and in my mind, I know them well. Just piqué, arabesque, chassé, step, leap; hands here, legs there, and repeat on the other side. My memory locked this in weeks ago, but my body has not caught up. My leg muscles tremble with the ineptness of a newborn giraffe. My arms flop around, seeking direction from my brain and receiving garbled, foreign messages in return. I've not been trained for this. Amy, Brie, Kait, and Paige have all been dancing for over a decade, and yet for some reason far from me, it is I chosen for this spotlight and not them.

As many girls do, I've stood in front of the mirror before, judging my every flaw. My ankles are blocks. My legs are short and twiggy. My shoulders bulge like every child's favorite sledding hill. Those thoughts crept into my consciousness, soaked with vanity. In these moments of piqué-arabesque-chassé-step-leap, I ponder similar thoughts—not of vanity—but of purpose. Now I wish my ankles and legs would be strong enough to sustain my weight when I repeatedly connect with the ground, which I cannot see or anticipate. I wish my shoulders carried the grace of a Russian ballerina or my body the picture of one who has worked hard for this position. I wish my arches did not ache after only two tries at this combination.

I try once more. Piqué: right ball of the foot planted, right arm up, left arm parallel to the ground. Arabesque: left leg straight behind, toe pointed. "You can do better than that," I tell myself. Chassé: a shuffle upstage, arms around an invisible basketball hoop. Step: knee bent to provide force upwards to help my partner lift me. I do not see him. Will he get to me in time? Will his arms be as strong as before? Will his fingers slip? Will our timing be synchronous?

Leap.

The piano continues playing, a slave to the metronome, but I do not hear it. The set below me stays in place, but I do not see it; its abrasive attack of new paint must be able to reach my nose, and yet I do not smell it. My partner's hands are steady on my waist, without which I would not be flying six feet in the air, but I do not feel them. There is another combination of steps to do once I land, but I do not think of them.

My body is the same inept form of bones and muscles it was before, yet in that moment I dance with the poise of an expert. I'm not a baby robin pushed from its nest; I am an eagle, strong and sure, soaring above a river. Suspended in the stratosphere all is calm, and I wish never to return to the hard ground below me.

But, as gravity has always deemed it, I must return. My head jerks back to the scene before me, and I comprehend the quick approaching ground. I'm suddenly reminded of early rehearsals, when my legs buckled beneath my weight because I forgot to do the simple task of looking from the space behind me to the oncoming floor. I once again fear the upcoming steps; they are the same as last time, but on the left side, which is inevitably more difficult. I leap on this side too, but I do not fly as I did before. Instead, I panic at the thought of my leg tensing instead of bending behind me into attitude, and how unrefined that must have looked to the audience.

When I finish, I know the steps were unsatisfactory, but they are done. Our moment ends, and we cross stage left. Fatigued, I fall into a chair just offstage, like a ballet slipper folded in half. The showy, fake smile fades from my face. I wish to be yet again suspended in midair, without a hip locked up in pain, or anatomy flash cards to memorize, or a text from my mother to answer. I wish to be a bird, above all the worries in the world.

An innocent eight-year-old runs up to me and says, "You are the bestest dancer I've ever seen," not knowing the aching muscles and weary mind found in that dancer. He sees in me everything I wish to be. He too is flying, with stars in his eyes, kept afloat by witnessing the marvel of his role models doing the incredible.

Josiah Lansford

Josiah Lansford is a dual-enrolled information technology management major from Jamestown, Ohio. He never considered writing as a talent before coming to Cedarville. When he is not playing the piano or practicing musical theatre, Josiah enjoys experimenting with the latest gadgets and riding his motorcycle.

Touching the Sky: Flying with Passion in the Face of Tragedy

It's hard to tell why I possess such an innate desire to fly. No prophecy was spoken over me at birth, nor was piloting a plane something I've always excelled at. Maybe I was just swept along with my family, following the wake of my predecessors. Yet I wonder if witnessing the cotton patchwork of clouds fall beneath my view influences my mind, rendering me unable to walk the earth without wistfully gazing towards the sky.

I cannot condense the narration of my literacy into a smooth chain of events but will instead record the narrative as it prevails in my mind, a mixed assortment of moments and images. While my experiences are unique to one man, the story they tell is universal. Growing up, I considered myself a participant in my surroundings. Little did I comprehend my experiences becoming part of me.

2005. "I'm leaving for work, see you when I get back." I feel my dad's bristly whiskers graze my cheek as he embraces his youngest son, punctuated by a peck on the cheek. He is embarking on the 4-hour commute to Detroit Metropolitan Airport, where he will strap himself in the cockpit of a pressurized aluminum cylinder and hurtle toward Europe through the upper atmosphere.

He will return in about a week, his flight bag bulging with streusel waffles, swiss cheese, and savory memories of his adventures abroad. Although my dad is gone a lot, having an airline pilot for a father carries its perks: Every summer, my family descends upon the Oregon Coast to visit relatives, receiving airline tickets at a heavy discount—provided there is room on the plane. Naturally, my favorite part is not the experience of flying, but the moment when the flight attendant shuffles down the aisle pushing a cart stocked with merrily clinking soda cans and small bags of salted pretzels for my indulgence. Over the years, the tired smell of the airport becomes my secondary home. Flying across the country at a moment's notice is something I take for granted.

    2008. The military speaker drones on. As I slouch back in my cold metal chair, my first thought is to inquire when lunch will be served. The sugary aroma of barbecue sloppy joes—in typical Army style—stirs my appetite. Suddenly, my last name thunders across the speakers, pulling me back to the present. I'm at a graduation ceremony, where my oldest brother Joel is to be awarded his army wings. My parents secure the pin to his lapel, and Joel is now a certified helicopter pilot in the Army. Though the prospect of lunch takes priority, I can't ignore the misty thought questioning what role aviation will play in my future.

    2013. "Okay Josiah, go ahead and open it!" I unwrap the gift for my birthday, careful not to tear the tissue-like paper. A black pilot's logbook appears. Written on the first of many clean pages is an entry for my recent flight with Joel in his small two-seater Cessna. As I stroke the dark, textured cover, a glowing sense of pride shines in my excited eyes. This logbook is a physical symbol of my yet unrealized future. I scrawl my name on the front page with black ink and carefully store the book in my dresser drawer. That first entry marks the start of my flight training and my development in the literacy of aviation.

One of the first competencies I tackle is how to safely land the plane. This is a difficult feat to master, and the first time the tricycle gear smacks down on the runway without assistance from the other seat I am ecstatic. This first clumsy maneuver, however, is far from perfect. Many more jolts onto the hard pavement and countless desperate calls by my father for more left rudder will be required before I grease the landing perfectly, a skill I continue to hone to the present day in preparation for my first solo flight.

As the busyness of high school devoured my spare time, the flight lessons in the following years grew relatively sporadic. Slowly, the aspiration of growing up to be a pilot faded from priority. During those few lessons, however, I developed a fundamental appreciation for the art of piloting an aircraft, and the skill and practice required to succeed. Little did I realize how deep this appreciation would eventually run. Though I knew that aviation was a core part of my family, I didn't understand until later that it had become part of me, too.

2015. November. I'm studying inside a university library, where the cold reality of class deadlines has pushed aside my dreamy thoughts of aviation. Suddenly, my phone buzzes. It's my oldest brother, Joel. He now flies corporate for a large company and wants to know if I would be interested in periodically detailing his plane. I would charge the same amount as the local airport's services but would have a much closer care to detail. "Absolutely."

Suddenly, I find myself lying on the chilled concrete floor of a large hangar, breathing in the syrupy smell of waterless cleaners as I scrub grease off the belly of a high-end single-engine Cirrus. Every week, microfiber cloth in hand, I knead the white and gray finish of the low wings to a reflective luster, vacuum every inch of the four leather seats, and carefully wipe the pristine fiberglass. Although I would much rather be flying the plane instead of cleaning it, the fact that I am working in a hangar filled with beautiful aircraft makes me grin, until overspray from my cleaning solution reminds me to keep my lips shut. Almost every good thing must come to an end, as they say, but many things aren't recognized for their true good until they do so.

2016. It is a cold, rainy night in January. The shivering clouds crumple together like a heavy quilt, and a persistent wind tumbles over the landscape. Judging from the weather, it would seem like a typical winter night, but tonight is anything but normal. At approximately 6:30 in the evening, a freshly-waxed Cirrus SR22 unexpectedly stalls on the final turn before landing and plunges into an embankment just short of Runway 25 at Greene County Regional Airport. The pilot is the sole occupant and is killed on impact. He is later identified as Joel Lansford.

My brother was taken doing the one thing he loved, and I am left behind questioning myself. Would it be proper to abandon aviation altogether as the loss of a family member through its grasp makes it too painful? Should one life stolen from my family be enough? Would continuing to pursue aviation in the face of death be irresponsible, or even worse, irreverent to the life that Joel lived?

Every cell in my body screams the contrary. No, the death of my brother makes the magnetic pull of the milky summer sky even more forceful. The color of aviation runs too thickly through my blood vessels to be extracted.

September. My dad—now retired and a licensed flight instructor—and I drive together to the old rusty hangar in Springfield. It's time to start flying again. For the first time in over a year, I perform the pre-flight walkaround inspection, checking for loose rivets in the high wings and running my hands over the two-bladed propeller. After pulling the plane out of the hangar, I climb into the cockpit, strap myself in, and place my hands on the controls. "Springfield traffic, this is Cessna eight-zero-seven-six-foxtrot, departing on Runway 24 and exiting the pattern to the southeast." As we rumble down the airstrip and lift off, I look over and see the creases from a big smile on my dad's cheeks. It's good to be back in the air.

Daniel Parschauer

Daniel Parschauer is a sophomore pharmacy major from Lancaster, PA. Although he has had his fair share of writing assignments, he has never considered himself a skilled writer. Outside of studying to become a pharmacist, he enjoys playing volleyball and spending time with friends and reading a good book.

Reminiscence of Home

It's no secret that college food is almost always awful, and this fact is proven true yet again today. I have just sat down at my previously saved seat in the cafeteria of our college. I make a brief and silent prayer and then look down at my food. How wonderful. A heap of droopy, shiny pizza, a bowl of mush trying to be chili, and a cup of apple juice. I'm definitely getting cereal after this. Eating a bowl of cereal after dinner ensures that I will leave at least somewhat satisfied with my meal. The cafeteria is alive with hungry students, and their individual voices are all contributing to the overarching jumble of sound. Several tables over, someone has burned something at the grill, as evidenced by the acrid smell that has reached my table. My hall mates trickle over to our table and initiate the normal jargon of a weekday dinner.

"How was your day?"
"Fine. I had two exams – that was fun."
"Dude, that sucks."
"Is anybody making a run to Walmart tonight?"
"What'd you think of the chapel speaker?"
"Yeah, I'm going to Walmart after dinner."

The conversations continue to roll, blending with one another until they coalesce with the hum of the crowds, and my mind begins to wander back to a time when I was home.

I have just returned from the grocery store down the road. After church that morning, Mom set to making dinner – what we called the Sunday after-church meal – and, as usual, made me a quick list of things to pick up for her. This time the list is relatively short: fat free ricotta, a loaf of French bread, and seltzer water for Dad. Victoriously carrying my two plastic bags, I enter our home. Mom is across the room at her stove stirring homemade gravy (marinara sauce with meatballs cooking in it) and tending to a pot of boiling water. The oven range fan is humming away as it collects steam from the twin pots. I can hear water spilling over the rim of its vessel and sizzling on the hot stove before evaporating – a sure sign that it's ready for whatever the choice pasta is. To my right the screen door is letting in a soft summer breeze that carries with it the ringing of wind chimes on our back porch. The scent of dark, nutty coffee drifts in the air. Mom probably brewed a pot for her and me to enjoy. The most overwhelming detail, however, is the smell of the gravy. The dramatic aroma is so strong that I can identify each ingredient in the sauce: fresh basil, parsley, and oregano from our garden, meatballs, olive oil, extra garlic for good measure, and a hint of Splenda to counter the acidic tomatoes. We always eat pasta on Sundays, just like Mom's family before us and her grandparents' before her. Tradition runs deep in Italian homes. Summer Sundays are extra special because we have dinner outside on the back deck.

  I walk into the kitchen and begin unpacking what I had bought, bragging about how I had picked the crispest loaf of bread they had. Just as I finish putting the ricotta in the fridge, my sister walks in from the garden, carrying under her arm a bowl of red, yellow, and purple tomatoes and sprigs of more basil. To take advantage of the massive harvest, Mom is making bruschetta to go with dinner, another classic. She offers me a mug of that coffee to pass the time. I take my usual seat for when I watch her cook: on the countertop opposite the stove. As predicted, the water is ready and Mom had selected ravioli. She pours them into the turbulent water and we begin to talk. The most meaningful conversations I've ever had with my mother take place in the kitchen. Perhaps it's because we are most comfortable here, or perhaps the hectic setting stimulates thoughtful topics. We picked out my tux for prom here. We figured out what my major in college would be here. We laughed over Mom's impersonation of Julia Child here and cried over my grandmother's death here. I can safely say that much of who I am has come out of this kitchen. Today the conversation is light, and we chat away while she cooks, losing track of time and enjoying each other's company. Unfortunately, the kitchen is no place to lose track of anything, and the ravioli boils over, leading Mom into a frenzy as she lowers the temperature and stirs the water to calm it down. Finally succeeding, she checks the sauce to make sure the taste is right and asks for my opinion on its flavor. My conclusion is that it needs more salt, which is usually the case since Mom has a perpetual fear of over-salting anything she makes. After settling the dispute, my two sisters and I begin setting the table. We use the glass plates and good set of silverware when we eat outside – another tradition. Between the three of us, the joint effort will only take a couple minutes.

  Just as we are bringing out the last few items, I hear the smoke alarm go off in the kitchen. Although unpleasant and piercingly loud, I'm not surprised. Mom is a fantastic cook, but it's not uncommon for her to accidentally fill the kitchen with smoke. In this case, meatball grease that had dripped out in the oven began to burn, and smoke poured out when Mom opened the oven door to put the bread in. "Hey, Bubba! Come turn the alarm off!" she yells above the ringing. "Coming!" Since I am the tallest person home, it's my responsibility to solve the problem, which I promptly do by removing the battery from the alarm. With it turned off, we continue with our work. Shortly after, I can hear the rhythmic thud of the garage door opening, and we all know Dad is home from church. As the pastor, it's normal for him to stay behind and talk to people well after the service is over. Our dog, a short and fat bolt of energy, rushes past us to greet him. Dad gets swept into the fray of finishing dinner when Mom asks him to retrieve the scolapasta – a massive strainer for pasta – from the pantry. With pride, Mom reminds us that you always know when ravioli is done cooking when they float to the surface.

    Finally, after much preparation, all of us are seated at the table. We fold our hands as Dad prepares to pray, but I take a moment to absorb the scene. It is a truly perfect day. The pergola my Dad and I built covers us in just the right amount of shade, keeping us neatly cool. Mom's flower beds surround the entire deck in a diverse palette of brilliant yellows, reds, pinks, and blues. The breeze is still mingling with the wind chimes, adding another line of notes to the already harmonious music of local birds. Behind me, cream colored curtains drift in the wind, contrasting perfectly with the deep chestnut of our deck. Before me, a flawless meal is sprawled out on the round table. Ravioli mixed with short, fingerlike cavatelli are displayed in a ceramic sky blue bowl, covered in red, steaming gravy. A white platter of fresh bruschetta sits next to it. We need to hurry and get to eating before the balsamic vinegar soaks through the bread. Immediately in front of me sits another bowl, this one filled with more sauce and meatballs.

Smaller bowls of ricotta, parmesan, and olives dot the table, available for anyone to help themselves to. Even though we eat this meal often, I am eager to dig in and taste everything all over again. Dad finishes his thoughtful prayer and we begin dinner. The following time would be full of cheerful conversation. My sisters would talk about the latest happenings on their favorite TV show. Mom would express her satisfaction with the latest results in the Presidential elections. Dad would tell his inspiring stories of ministry at church, and I would sit back and take it all in, enjoying the company of my family.

    All is as it should be. Food is on the table, and my family is together with me. But suddenly they aren't. The songs of birds are replaced by the scooting of chairs, the warm sun by cold fluorescent lights, and my family by my hall mates. I find myself once again in the campus cafeteria. My friends are ready to return to our dorm, and everybody is getting up and putting on their coats. I quickly return to reality to join them, but reflect on my memories. How curious it is that the past is draped in a golden light. Moments of joy are exaggerated for fondness' sake while hints of reality are quietly tucked away. Will I look on this current time – walking through a cafeteria after a disappointing meal with friends – with the same ideality as I have just now looked at home? I suppose the creation of memory warped by wishful thinking is the device by which we continue to enjoy the past. Nevertheless, I will remember the home I am most fond of because it is these memories that I enjoy most.

Aubrey Podnar

Aubrey Podnar is a freshman nursing major from Akron, Ohio. She enjoys language and descriptive writing. Aubrey's interests include drawing, playing sand volleyball, and riding horses.

How
Idiopathic Juvenile Osteoporosis
Will Not Ruin
Your Life;
Also How God Can Turn
Your Pain to Joy:
A memoir

In the third grade I went to
The doctor's for an x-ray of
My lungs. They were looking
To improve my vocal cord
Dysfunction, but instead
Found two fractures in my
spine. My T7 and T8 vertebrae
Were misshapen. I was forbid
From playing any contact
Sports, which meant for me
No more soccer or horseback
Riding. As an active nine-year-
Old girl I was devastated to have
My favorite things taken away
From me. I was not allowed to
Participate in the normal gym
Class activities, for fear of further

Injuring my back. Self-esteem is
Crucial in a girl's adolescent years,
And mine plummeted after this
Revelation. I grew unsure of
Myself and doubted my self
Worth. From birth to my fifth
Birthday I had unwillingly
Succumbed to seven seizures,
And my vocal chord dysfunction
Made me wheeze like your average
Asthmatic. To top off the new
Knowledge that my spinal cord was
Missing pieces, I was transferring
Schools. Elementary school is crucial
For developing friendships, and I did
Not know a single soul at my new school.
I was the freak with the back brace.
However, I was not alone. There were
Other children who could not play
In gym class with everyone else either.
I showed up on my first day of gym time,
And I saw my future. I was no longer the
weird new girl with spine problems who
had to drink   glasses
of milk at all of her meals, the child
Wearing the   ugly
Beige back brace contraption, swallowing
pills the size of Texas. I was just
Another student in gym class, trying
To make it around the gym on the

Specially crafted tricycles. My new
Gym classmates were the occupants
Of the special needs classroom at the
End of the hall: as a third grader, they
Were already known as the weird kids.
Now I was a weird kid as well. I knew there
Was something about them that was different,
And I also knew as an innocent nine-year
Old that Jesus calls us to love everyone.
So I tried to ignore the reproaches of the other
Students and I got to know my new friends
As we spent an hour together each day. Over
The next three years, some of my best friends
Struggled with Autism and Williams syndrome.
We would play together on the playground, share
Meals together in a cramped lunchroom, but our
Gym time together was unique. It was where we
grew together, laughed together, got frustrated
Together, learned together.
It seems inconsequential, a recounting of a
Third grade girl's experience with a minor
Back injury. 'Tis a woeful tale of misfortune starring
A middle child from a middle class suburban
family. But I believe that my close relationship
with a mentally disabled elementary class gave
Me new eyes. Getting to know those children
As a child myself gave me an appreciation for how
Diversely we have all been created, and how similar
We are to one another. The one characteristic that
Bonds us together is that we were all formed by the

Most imaginative Creator. No matter how quickly
Your brain develops, your genetics, or at what level
you function, we are all created in Christ's image.
I learned pretty quickly how cruel people can be.
With my own abnormalities, I felt a fraction of
My friends' pain. Long after I outgrew my own
Osteoporosis, I thought about my time with the
Special needs class, and I decided that I wanted
To make my experience a part of my future. I
Chose to pursue nursing to help people feel
Valued. No child should have to grow up
Thinking they are alone in their struggles.
Through my own physical pain and
Emotional turbulence, I learned that every
Person has a place in God's kingdom. We
All were created with purpose, and I
Wish to spread that message to the
Ill and broken people throughout
The world. I have a special place
In my heart for the mentally
Disabled, people who may believe
They are not worth much in
Today's chaotic society.
"But even the hairs of
Your head have all
Been numbered.
Fear not; you are
More valuable
Than many
Sparrows."

Luke 12:7
I am a
Child
Of
God.

Psalm 139:13-14

"For you formed my inward parts; you knitted me together in my mother's womb. I praise you, for I am fearfully and wonderfully made. Wonderful are your works; my soul knows it very well."

Kimberly Powell

Kimberly Powell is a freshman marketing major from Ohio. She loves creative writing and often journals before she hits the pillow each night. A blonde from a family of five daughters, Kimmy enjoys whistling, playing volleyball, and meeting new people. Her enthusiasm and energy shines through her every laugh and smile. Kimmy loves the Lord with all her heart and sharing Christ's love by encouraging those around her.

Blank Pages, Colorful Thoughts

"But Mrs. Connolly, I'm stumped. I have no clue what to write," I complained as my fellow classmates began to scribble away on yellow steno pads. She peered overtop her brown-rimmed glasses and smiled as she replied, "Then write just that. All I want you to do is to transfer the thoughts in your head onto the paper in front of you." She clapped her hands together a couple times as she made her way back to a steaming cup of coffee waiting at her desk. Directing my attention back to the blue lines, I began to write. *Umm, well, I'm writing right now, and I had waffles for dinner last night.* Incoherent thought bled into the next incoherent thought, but nonetheless, I was writing. Meanwhile, the wall commonly known as "writer's block" slowly began to crumble as my inner creative monster broke into my imagination.

Minutes later, Mrs. Connolly slipped on her heeled boots and made her way to the podium in the front of the classroom. Her short stature, even though she walked in 3-inch wedges, was unthreatening, comical even, and her voice was lively as she exclaimed, "Alright, pencils down. Who wants to read first?" Hands popped up all around the room, waving frantically in hopes being the first to tell his or her story, but my hands remained securely underneath my thighs as I slid further down in my seat. My best friend Mollie turned to me and said, "Oh, come on Kimmy! Why don't ya wanna read?" Before I could respond, she raised her left hand as she nervously chewed on her right hand's nails. Because of her unmatched enthusiasm, Mrs. Connolly called on Mollie, who cleared her throat before beginning in a high-pitch, yet cheerful tone. Her blue eyes widened with each added description, and as I sat amongst her classmates, laughing at Mollie's inflection in the differing characters and well-timed jokes, I could not help being impressed by the random creativity she had stored in the crevices of her brain.

 My eyes returned to my own writing, and the moments of creative revelation I had had minutes before seemed to dull in comparison to the originality Mollie presented in the matter of seconds. Unlike my best friend, the box that withheld my creativity, my independent thinking had yet to be opened, but over the course of my middle school years, the tape slowly but surely was ripped off, revealing originality that shaped me into who I am today.

 Every morning, promptly at 9:02 Mrs. Connolly would walk to the front of the classroom, grab a colored expo marker, and write a prompt on the whiteboard. I would stare at the options, quickly formulating mini stories around each one and choosing the one I thought most relatable. When pen met paper, I found it difficult to begin, to string my thoughts together in such a way as to entertain my classmates and express the creativity stored deep in my brain. Countless times, I would begin a sentence only to scratch it out upon losing a train of thought. Each sentence seemed boring and bland in comparison to Mollie's. Somehow, she was like a master chef when it came to writing: she enticed listeners with a drizzling of gerunds and dialogue, spiced up the plot with grueling actions and tasteful adjectives, and left them with a nail-biting cliffhanger. My stories, on the other hand, were the equivalent to toast: plain, white, flavorless toast.

In hopes of gaining the appetites of my listeners, I asked Mollie one day how she was such a good writer. "I dunno, Kim. I just kinda write what I'm thinking," she said as she tilted her head to the side, letting out an innocent little giggle. I picked up my pencil but remained motionless as I stared at the blank sheet before me. In the upper left corner I wrote the word The; hesitating, I began to erase that single word, but the lead merely smeared, so I tore the page from my notebook and scrunched it into a small ball. When I knew Mrs. Connolly had turned around, I shot the paper ball into the nearby wastebasket. Hearing the sound of the plastic trash bag, she whipped around in her chair and stared at me overtop those brown-rimmed glasses. Like a guilty puppy, I slinked back in my seat, monotonously tapping my number two pencil against my wooden desk. Despite my many attempts, I could find no perfect way to start my story, and and instead of brainstorming ideas, I crossed out the words, obliterating any trace of my failed efforts.

Mrs. Connolly, wise with many years, sensed that I was struggling, and sat down with me after class. The joints in the student desk creaked as she eased into the plastic seating. My eyes remained locked on the scratched out words and phrases on the page in front of me. The ticking clock in the front of the classroom echoed as we sat in the silence. I took in a deep breath, inhaling the smells of old, used books and then exhaled. Without looking up from my journal, I muttered, "I am so boring. This journaling comes so easily for Mollie, but when I try to be funny or serious, it doesn't sound good." Quiet for a moment, Mrs. Connolly crossed her arms and placed her hand under her chin as if to emphasize the fact that she was thinking. "Kimmy," she replied, resting her hand gently on my shoulder. "I think you just need to find your voice, not Mollie's voice or anyone else's but your very own unique voice."

My own voice. Up until that point, my writing had merely been a regurgitation of facts, a replication of sentences I had seen in children's books, a daily chore for learning parts of speech. But writing is so much more than that. Mrs. Connolly, interrupting the motion of the wheels turning in my head, said, "Kimmy, tell me a story. Any story." I thought for a moment and instantly remembered a comical instance that had happened at recess the day before. As I recounted the story, a smile began to appear on Mrs. Connolly's face. "There you go!" she exclaimed. "That is your voice. Now just write those words down on paper."

Something clicked within me. It was as if my thoughts had gone from black and white to vibrant HD color, as if my imagination had come alive on paper. Writing, among many things, was a means of thinking aloud, a way for my God-given creativity to be expressed. I sat in the grey, plastic chair in the middle of the classroom, thinking about the hundreds of worlds my pencil had yet to explore. Closing my steno pad, I turned to Mrs. Connolly and grinned from ear to ear. "You're the best, Mrs. C." Her blue eyes sparkled with what I thought was a tear, and her warm smile appeared once again. "I'll see ya tomorrow, kiddo," she replied as she returned to her desk.

Each day in 6th grade English seemed better than the one before. My love for creative writing was poured into journals both at school in my locker and at home on my nightstand. I had found my voice and with each passing day, that voice grew louder and stronger. When Mrs. Connolly would ask for volunteers to read, my hand was one of the first to shoot up. As I read my stories, the class seemed to melt over the fire that my creativity had set. Within a matter of sentences, I had gripped the attention of the audience, taking them with me on my journeys as a CIA agent and as an orphaned monkey. Even Mollie, whom I had hailed a child prodigy in the area of creative writing, once whispered to me after I read my story, "Kimmy, that story was hilarious!" A goofy grin crossed her face as she winked in my direction. I giggled back, "Thanks," as we high-fived and sat back in our chairs. Mrs. Connolly, who surely had the hearing of a bat, seemed to have heard the interaction that Mollie and I just shared because instead of reprimanding our giggling, she simply flashed the same warm smile and continued on with her lesson. From then on, a permanent warm smile was etched on my face. I absolutely loved writing, and more than anything, I wanted to share that love with more than just those in my class.

    Going into high school, my sphere of influence drastically changed from nine kids and a handful of teachers at a Christian school to well over a thousand kids at the local high school. Much of my freshman year I shied away from the creativity scene, keeping many of my stories and ideas to myself. Hankering for a creative outlet, I decided to make a scrapbook for my sister that summer through a program in 4H. I soon found that unlike writing, scrapbooking told a story through pictures and artsy stickers and embellishments, giving me the artistic license to be innovative, to think outside the limitation of words, and to take crafting to a whole new level. But much like the writing process, it was not easy to scrapbook. Countless nights I stared at yet another blank paper, only this time, a colored pattern decorated the page. The pictures and stickers served as the words of my story, and after arranging and rearranging them at different angles, my glue gun, acting as my pencil, would commit my words to paper.

When the day came for judging, the gray-haired woman fingered through the glossy pages, analyzing the fine-tuned details and the colorful decorations. She paused only to push her glasses back up the bridge of her nose as she continued to flip through the pages. After waiting patiently for a response, I asked her, "Well? What do you think?"

She smiled, the same reassuring smile I had seen countless times before on Mrs. Connolly's face after she had listened to one of my stories. "This is a story," the woman began, "that I think the judges at the Ohio State Fair would like to see." Dumbfounded, I stammered over my words, forcing out a quick thank you before running to tell my mother the good news.

For three years, judges at the Ohio State Fair viewed my artwork. They took the time, whether they liked it or not, to listen to my voice, a voice which for so long struggled to be heard. A voice, which found it difficult to sing in the quiet moments. A voice which, given time, would reveal a creativity that would otherwise have remained silent, dormant in my mind. A voice, which was finally heard because of woman's ability to inspire.

Presley-Peyton Shemelia

Presley-Peyton Shemelia is a freshman social work major from Philadelphia, PA. She does not typically share her writing with others but has enjoyed composition and found writing this piece to be one of the most challenging moments of her freshman career. When she is not doing school work, Presley-Peyton enjoys playing piano, fellowshipping with others, and spending time outdoors.

The Art of Crying

I sit alone, curled up in a crooked lump with my back pushed against the icy whitewashed wall. I try to become invisible and cease to exist, but everything in my body is telling me that I am still here. Still breathing. My hands shake like my gentle grandfather who had Parkinson's and my heart pounds faster than it did the day I received my first kiss. My lungs struggle to force oxygen into my body without making the slightest noise that would give my emotions away. *The first tear begins to form.*

Desperately, I try to squeeze my eyes shut in an attempt to suppress the ocean that is about to demolish its barriers. I know that when the first tear falls the struggle will be over, but I do not surrender because I am not convinced I can live with this grief. I do not want to admit that he is gone. My body starts to rock back and forth, imitating a mother soothing her distressed child. I tell myself I will not give in, I will not accept today, and I will not allow myself to feel the weight of tears. I know the barriers are beginning to crack because my eyelids sense moisture. This dampness exhilarates my body putting all my senses on high alert. Suddenly I am aware of the rough carpet my feet have been drilled into and the crumpled pile of laundry full of blacks and grays that sits under me. I hear the buzzing of air circulating in the room and can barely sense the vibration of the fan sitting across from me. I smell the familiar scent of my quiet place which always reminds me of a field of wild flowers.

A new discovery commands the attention of my senses as I feel a cool droplet begin to pave its course down my cheek and past my crooked nose. I can feel it reach the end of my chin and watch the tear land on my green Eagles shirt, green having always been my grandfather's favorite color. Then another droplet begins to form and my crimson red cheeks are astonished by the cold sensation overcoming my heated face. I give in and let the tears fall one by one as I take in the dreaded moisture I have been fighting. Each tear that falls strips away another piece of my hard façade I held together for so long. I feel the relieving sense of no longer pushing back the overwhelming waters and I begin to doubt my anxieties wondering why I was so scared to feel the soothing sensation of tears and the relief that letting go brings.

The tears thoroughly soak through my tattered shirt as I feel my body calming down. My lungs begin to take in proper amounts of oxygen and my heart rate slows to a steady thump. My throat no longer burns from gasping for air and the shaking in my hands subside. I begin wiping off the water that has now engulfed my face but quickly give up as it just begins to cover my arms. My feet extend from their cramped position and my back straightens itself out. A calm washes over me and I sit in silence until the last tear escapes and no more fall. I hesitantly rise to my feet and am faced with my image in the mirror.

I look different than when I first entered the room. My emotions are no longer hidden under a perfectly contoured face and my crimson red cheeks are now a soft cherry color. My eyes are still moist, but the deep sorrow that made them appear near black has been replaced with a mahogany brown that seems to invite others in. My hair is no longer in its tight braid, but it envelops my face, telling the story of surrender. I finally realize that crying stripped away the hardened persona I tried to put on and revealed the helpless girl in need of a friend who no longer wants to bear the weight of sorrow alone. As I begin the process of washing off my tears and pulling my hair back into an orderly braid my mind wonders. I think of others who will experience the renewal crying brings and wonder what color their soaked shirts will be or what their tear stained faces will reveal to them.

Johnna Willis

Spiritual Training

Dozens have told me their story. I've heard of some coming to know Christ at age five and others not meeting him until they were gray. My story follows more closely to the former yet applies to my life every day while studying for my degree. From the time I was born until now in college, experiences and people have trained me to be the person and teacher God calls me to be.

I spent my time growing up singing off-key, giggling frequently, playing in the dirt, jumping off swings, and hearing scripture from my family. My dad was the youth pastor at a nearby Baptist church in Southern West Virginia where he lived the gospel inside and out of the youth rooms. From the time I could speak I could repeat bible verses and answer foundational questions such as "What is sin?" like a robot. My parents would ask me questions and I would generate the best answer a child could give.

This routine and heartless knowledge continued as such until I attended one of my church's outreaches directed by my dad. The children's program consisted of people of all ages shouting and cheering for their own designated team. There, I could be the crazy, energetic kid I was at home. At the end of the night, everything calmed down. My dad told the hundred or more students the story from John 3 of Nicodemus coming to Jesus at night. In verse 3 of the passage, Jesus tells Nicodemus that in order to go to heaven he must be "born again." When he finished speaking there was an invitation to accept Christ. I didn't understand what being "born again" meant for me, so I went to the back to speak with a leader about it and ended up receiving Christ.

Although it was a memorable and celebrated night, little changed after I became a Christian. My family always attended church, prayed, and encouraged personal devotions and Christ-like influences. However, the older I got, the more in-depth my devotions became and the more questions I asked others and myself.

One day that stands out in my Christian life is September 14th, 2012. That day I checked a Christian radio station's website and on the sidebar they advertised for King & Country's newly released music video for their song, "The Proof of Your Love." The cover art intrigued me with black and white, strange "uniforms" on adults and children, and dark, eerie eyes. I had heard the song once or twice beforehand, but after only watching the video once it ended up on repeat for the next few days. The newly-featured band told the story of a child who was beaten for speaking up in a prison about the love of Christ. The men who heard him speak carefully spread the news throughout the prison. The zombie-like people within the walls came alive as the good news spread, but the men sharing the news were thrown into cells and hurt for not following routine.

This jarred some questions concerning my faith. I didn't know if I had the trust in God to spread His love when times were hard. I didn't think I could withstand persecution if it ever came. I couldn't see myself being the person to risk it all to tell others the good news like the men did in the music video. I watched the video over and over until I came to tears before God and told him I wanted him to rule over everything. My comfort wasn't mine, my friendships weren't mine, and my schoolwork wasn't mine.

High school tested my priorities. I had made decisions to trust God through it all but I wasn't succeeding in keeping up with them. Thankfully, God placed two wonderful young ladies in my path, Liza and Kristen. Liza worked at my Summer camp and Kristen became like my big sister within our church. As I struggled in high school, they struggled in college, but I saw they handled greater loads of stress more gracefully than I did because they relied on God over themselves. They taught me about serving God in everything and using my talents to bring him glory. Kristen told me, "Learning and studying is an act of worship because it's something that the Lord intended for us. It, by definition, is good when the purpose of it is to bring God glory or enable us to serve Him better."

I spoke to Liza about how she stayed motivated through difficult classes. She replied with, "I was convinced... to take my studies more seriously for the sake of the Gospel. So, really, I guess my intention became to rely on Jesus to be my motivation and encourager throughout school." She also reminded me of Colossians 3:17 which says, "And whatever you do, whether in word or deed, do it all in the name of the Lord Jesus, giving thanks to God the Father through him."

Words like Liza's from multiple other strong influences helped me through high school and into college. Some high school classes seemed useless in many ways, but college classes often related to my major. I chose the major that Kristen and my mother both pursued: Early Childhood Education. One reason I chose to become a teacher was to be a missionary to my own classroom, but first, I had to become a Christ-like example in my own studies.

My connection with God first occurred when I was the age of my future students, therefore I know personally they can be impacted. My decision to dedicate everything to Christ will apply to my future career in the public school system. These two experiences in my past continue to impact my studying to be an educator. However, I know before I can become a Christ-like teacher I must keep my studies Christ-like.

I know my purpose at school is to learn to be an outstanding teacher from my professors and courses. Proverbs 22:6 says, "Train a child in the way he should go, and when he is old he will not turn from it." My training began at a young age, and thanks to experiences and mentors I had growing up, I felt spiritually strengthened for challenges to come.

Works Cited Page

(Bordanada, L., personal communication, September 8, 2016)

(Loveday, K., personal communication, September 8, 2016)

Richards, L., & Richards, S. P. (2009). Holy Bible. Grand Rapids, MI: Zondervan

Analysis

Andrew Bidlen
Abigail Brighton
Sharri Hall
Connor Tomlin Haynes
Lila Pattison
Kimberly Powell

Andrew Bidlen

Andrew Bidlen is a senior electrical engineering major from North Royalton, OH. He is passionate about using technology to empower data-driven decision making in the field of robotics and data science. He loves to play beach volleyball, go fishing, and hike. After graduation he plans to move to Charleston, SC with his wife Becky.

Robots Guide to Ethical Marketing

The 2005 animated film *Robots* captivated audiences by telling the story of Rodney Copperbottom, a small-town inventor turned world-changer. Rodney's journey from growing up in quiet Rivet Town to fighting for change in bustling Robot City illustrates the film's most obvious message, that everyone should tenaciously pursue their dreams. While this message is valuable, the film makes other significant claims about the real world. Most notably, the movie comments on the ethics of a prevalent real-world approach to marketing, which the movie embodies with the slogan "why be you when you can be new?" Rodney spends his time in Robot City battling against profit-hungry reformers trying to change the way that Bigweld Industries does business. *Robots* condemns corporations whose marketing claims that the personhood of consumers relies on the consumption of their product.

Robots demonizes characters who advocate for marketing strategies that tie personhood to the ownership of a product and glorifies those who do not. Rodney's heroic status is earned by his fight against Ratchet's attempt to force robots to rely on his product. Ratchet is portrayed as evil from the start when he holds a board meeting introducing his slogan "Why be you when you can be new?" As a board member disagrees with him, he dramatically ejects her from the building with a bout of evil laughter. Audience distaste for him only grows as the movie continues to portray him as a classic villain. His shiny "upgraded" body is a nod to his fake being. His reliance on his mother furthers audience perception of him as spineless. His mother, Madame Gasket, is depicted as evil by her rusty, dirty appearance and hostile treatment of employees. The audience first sees her feigning generosity by giving her workers a two-second break time. This mother-son duo, the masterminds behind the evil marketing scheme, are portrayed as the least likeable characters in the movie. Conversely, Rodney's dad and "outmode" friends are glorified for their positive outlook, even in dire circumstances. Herb is portrayed as a consistently hardworking and supporting husband and father. Throughout Rodney's childhood, Herb encourages him to follow his dreams by supporting his tinkering, even when it goes awry. Fender and Piper share what little they have with Rodney to make his trip to the big city more comfortable. The film portrays Rodney and the rest of the "good guys" as victimized by Ratchet, further demonizing Ratchet as a corporate leach.

Bigweld, the primary dynamic character throughout the movie, is most glorified when fighting against Ratchet's greedy scheme. Early in the movie, the audience sees Bigweld as an inspiration to robots everywhere. His introduction occurs as a float of his figure whizzes by Rodney and his father at a parade. Herb tells his son that Bigweld is "the greatest robot in the world", explaining that he invents things that make everyone's life better. Bigweld is glorified as the head of a company who relies on their customers to flourish. His slogan of "You can shine no matter what you're made of" resonates with many robots, including Rodney.

Later, when Rodney travels to meet Bigweld in Robot City, Bigweld is taken off his pedestal when he ignores Rodney's plea for help. His likeability is at an all-time low until he agrees to help Rodney several scenes later. Bigweld's change of heart comes after realizing that Ratchet's actions are wrong and need to be fought. By glorying Bigweld when he is most opposed to Ratchet's approach to business, the movie takes a clear stance in opposition of a company trying to convince customers that they are less if they do not purchase the company's product.

    Ratchet's marketing strategy hurts business by alienating two large groups of customers—those who cannot afford the product and those who resent the company's willing devaluation of non-customers. The movie opposes Ratchet's approach by exaggerating one of its major shortcomings; it inherently turns off customers. People who cannot afford to purchase the product feel devalued without any control over it. Fender, Piper, and the other outmodes embody this demographic in the movie. Purchasing Ratchet's upgrades is not an option for them, so they resent being belittled for something outside of their control. A different group of potential customers resent a company telling consumers that they need the company's product on ethical grounds and will boycott that company. Cappy, a clearly well-off board member of Bigweld industries helps Rodney and friends fight Ratchet in hopes of protecting the world from his deception. Losing this group of consumers is potentially more painful for the company because they actually had the means to purchase the product. The movie represents Ratchet's strategy as raising profits per sale slightly, but significantly decreasing the number of sales and therefore hurting revenue.

Robots demonstrates that a company can flourish without unethical marketing strategies by displaying the success of Bigweld Industries' positive business mantra "You can shine no matter what you're made of." This approach clearly contrasts Ratchet's marketing that relies on the insecurity and devaluation of the customer. The movie depicts two versions of Bigweld Industries, one that prioritizes the customer, promoting self-worth, and another that prioritizes profits over people. While the latter approach is clearly condemned, the former is portrayed as a viable alternative. Bigweld's notoriety as a Walt Disney-like character would be impossible without his company being successful first. Bigweld's notoriety is reiterated throughout the movie, first through his parade float and later through his starring TV role. The movie highlights the loyalty that his customers feel towards him and Bigweld Industries, a rare but desirable spot for a company to be in. The movie highlights Bigweld Industries effectiveness at reaching nearly all demographics. Literally every robot in the movie outside of Ratchet and his mother supports Bigweld's customer-first business model. The movie glorifies this model by portraying a smaller-profit, higher volume approach as equally or more profitable then Ratchet's plan to receive greater profit from a select few.

The movie exposes the lie behind Ratchet's marketing scheme in a single scene. Near the end of the movie, Rodney and his outmode friends are gathered in Madame Gasket's Chop Shop to fight Ratchet and his army. As the battle nears its end, it is increasingly clear that Rodney will be victorious. As this happens, Ratchet is shown as increasingly weak and timid. He is laughably spooked several times by plungers whizzing by or fallen comrades. This character transformation reaches its climax as he is snared in a web of chains and his shiny upgrades clatter to the floor. He is left dangling helplessly, and deflates with a cry of "Aah, my upgrades." It is very evident that he perceived his worth as tied to his upgrades and appearance, but at the end, they were worthless and could not save him. In contrast, it is this very moment that gives Rodney and his friends victory, clearly juxtaposing the world views of these characters.

  The claim that *Robots* makes about business is directly translatable to the real world. Many of the most powerful companies today take Ratchet's approach to marketing in their advertisements. Television commercials and radio ads often attempt to convince consumers that their state of being is dependent on purchasing the company's product. While this strategy is common in nearly every sector, it's especially glaring in make-up marketing. Maybelline poses the question "Maybe she's born with it, maybe it's Maybelline," directly implying that their product is needed to supplement a woman's natural appearance. While many see through these ads, others buy into their message, as indicated by the longevity of the strategy. This marketing approach does not align with a Biblical worldview. Companies who use this tactic are attempting to portray their products as a savior. This paves the way for idolatry and is clearly not a Biblical approach to marketing. *Robots* and the Bible agree, companies should rely on their customers, not vice versa.

Abigail Brighton

Abigail Brighton hails from Lancaster, PA and is a sophomore nursing major. She is not a natural writer but tries her best. She loves her nephew, volunteering at the fire station, playing volleyball, and Jesus.

Catching Flowers off Choctaw Ridge

The Mississippi sun was shining when Bobbie Gentry, a typical Southern farmer's daughter, received news about her lover that would cause an emotional storm to her routine life. She would have never expected such a tragedy to wreck her life and leave her all alone. In her musical hit, "Ode to Billie Joe," Gentry describes her experience hearing about her boyfriend committing suicide by jumping off the Tallahatchie Bridge on Choctaw Ridge. Her family's unconcerned reactions further complicate the situation and deprive Gentry of the community she needs to grieve the tragedy in a healthy manner. "Ode to Billie Joe" suggests that people should interrupt their lives to empathize with others yet often fail to do so because they fear the suffering that will inevitably come their way.

Bobbie Gentry uses irony in the lack of lyrics about Billie Joe to provide evidence for the selfishness of people refusing to disturb their lives with empathy. Typically, odes express the memory of someone else, but in this case, less than half of the lyrics recall Billie Joe. Common life occurrences, such as eating dinner or daily work, take precedence over the boy's death and distract the family from recognizing the seriousness of Billie Joe's actions. Although the song is called an "ode," the lyrics do not revolve around the boy in the title, but instead, around his lover's experience. This truth leads to fact that the singer herself refuses to empathize with how Billie Joe must have been struggling, signifying a human pattern to deny empathy even to loved ones. While Gentry refuses to express the pain of her lover, her family also denies empathy for her. With subtlety, the family members mention Gentry as the lover of Billie Joe but ignore the obvious emotional turmoil of the singer. They speak revealing comments such as, "And wasn't I talkin' to him last Sunday night?" and "he saw a girl that looked a lot like you... and she and Billie Joe was throwing somethin' off the Tallahatchie Bridge." The singer's loved ones speak these casual comments without any concern for the impact of this event on Bobbie Gentry, leaving her to cope alone as she refuses to eat and spends an unduly amount of time throwing flowers over the bridge where Billie Joe jumped. The denial of empathy and consideration for others leads to a broken community, as exhibited by the singer and her lover, as well as the singer and her family.

    The monotonous strumming and lyrical repetition throughout "Ode to Billie Joe" emphasizes the single-minded lifestyle that denies any action to look to others and help in community. Initiated before the start of Bobbie Gentry's lyrics, the strumming pattern creates a continuous dull, sad mood, repeating throughout the entire song and pausing only at the end of each stanza to state, "Billie Joe's jumped off the Tallahatchie Bridge." At this point in the song, the strumming stops and the only music is Gentry singing this statement and a cello bowing low, dramatic notes. As soon as she expresses the news of his tragedy, the strumming once again continues as though the death of Billie Joe indicates no significance. This pattern directly reflects the theme of the song: People have their own lives and responsibilities apart from others and do not want to interrupt their own life patterns, putting themselves at risk for emotional suffering. Like the motif of the guitar, people want their lives to continue as before despite the misfortune of others. Each time the strumming picks up after the depressing statement, the family members make a subconscious rejection of empathy and fall back to old life patterns.

Each stanza describes the fear of a different family member to allow himself to empathize with the suffering of the singer. Each passes judgement to Billie Joe and denies any remorse or validation to who he was as a person. With such reactions, they separate themselves from acknowledging the importance of the event, leaving Bobbie Gentry without support in her grief. The first character to speak is Papa. He is clearly not interested in Choctaw Ridge for he says, "Seems like nothin' ever comes to no good up on Choctaw Ridge." He then judges the boy saying, "Well, Billie Joe never had a lick of sense." This judgement is a refusal to provide empathy for the boy, but more than that, he has the first speaking point and the leadership role in the family. As the head of this traditional family, making such statements limits conversations that could have happened at the dinner table to promote support for his struggling daughter. Unfortunately, he has already invalidated the event with these two statements.

Also fearful of hindering his own life routine, Bobbie Gentry's brother focuses on himself rather than give attention to his sister. He follows his father's cue by only briefly recalling a memory with Billie Joe and quickly moving on to ask for another piece of pie. Even as a friend of Billie Joe, he offers minimal empathy in the statement, "it don't seem right." The event does not impact him deeply like his sister, as obvious in the fact that he gets married, buys a store and moves away—all within the year.

Bobbie Gentry's mother also has all the evidence she needs to see her daughter's relationship to the boy, yet fails to acknowledge the effects of this tragedy on Bobbie Gentry. With previous cues from her son, she continues to speak as if nothing happened, asking Bobbie Gentry, "Child, what's happened to your appetite? ... you haven't touched a single bite." The mother even states that the preacher had come because he had seen the two together but still blatantly chooses selfishness over her daughter's reality. The mother's priorities are that the preacher is coming over for dinner and not that the two were seen together, as evident in the order that the mother talks about her and the preacher's conversation. The song suggests that the preacher wants to offer support, yet her mother refuses to recognize the importance of support in her daughter's life. Gentry's mother also uses casual language throughout the discussion such as, "oh, by the way…". This indicates the ignorance in her mother's view of the significant tragedy. Following in her mother's footsteps, Bobbie Gentry will also later deny empathy for her mother after her father's death, thus creating a cycle of broken community.

This lack of community for Bobbie Gentry gives significance to the song as a solo, rather than a duet. It would be contradictory for the song to be a duet since the singer's lover has just died and left Bobbie Gentry alone—her brother married and moved away, her father dead and her mother so depressed that she will not do anything, which also indicates the implications of living without empathy. As explained in the family's reaction to the tragedy of Billie Joe, such life without expressed empathy creates emotional and relational separation, destroying kinship. Without this community, people will end up like mother and Bobbie Gentry, alone and wallowing in their grief.

The mournful tone of the song expresses emotional turmoil that results because of the fear to be vulnerable with empathy when hearing the news of Billie Joe's suicide. The string instrumentals add build with long, dramatic mellow-sounding notes each time the song mentions the Tallahatchie Bridge. At the end of "Ode to Billie Joe," the singer finally hints at her relationship with Billie Joe when she throws flowers off the bridge, just as her brother mentioned Billie Joe and her doing before Billie Joe's death. The strings at this point perform an intense chromatic scale, concluding the song and attributing final emotion to the overall story as the audience ponders the implications of the song. The sadness provokes thought about what community could have been for Bobbie Gentry and her family if they would have listened to each other's emotions and supported each other through suffering.

"Ode to Billy Joe" reveals the tendency for people to destroy community by ignoring the misfortune of others because of a selfish fear of the effect that empathy will have on them. Without the support of others, one can remain in the depression state in the grieving process. Bobbie Gentry's family is an excellent example of what would happen if humans refused to acknowledge and assist in one another's suffering. This message is not only evident in the failure of some to fully recover from tragic life events, but to be in community is also a Biblical directive. In Hebrews 10:24, God instructs His children, "And let us be concerned about one another in order to promote love and good works…encouraging one another" (Holman Christian Standard Bible, Hebrews 10:24). As God teaches in His Word, the human community has the capability of moving past many hardships to live out productive, happy, relational lives that encourage and build each other through hard times. One can accomplish this by validating each other's emotions and recognizing misfortune. In a symbolic sense, loved ones should be there for each other to catch the flowers that may be thrown off the Tallahatchie Bridge on Choctaw Ridge.

Works Cited

The Bible. Holman Christian Standard Bible, Holman Bible Publishers, 2012.

Bobbie Gentry. "Ode to Billie Joe." *Ode to Billie Joe*, Capitol Records, 1967, *Spotify.*

Sharri Hall

An Analysis of Luke Redd on Free Higher-Education

The debate on free higher-education presents significant polarization. In his article on *Tradeschools, Colleges, and Universities*, Luke Redd seeks to present arguments for and against free higher-education and have readers decide upon which side of the debate they will stand. He believes the topic deserves "an open mind and a balanced exploration of the potential benefits, drawbacks, and alternatives."

Luke Redd gives arguments for and against free higher-education and offers arguments to a middle-ground which he calls "alternatives." Unfortunately, Redd does not present arguments for any side well. Though he offers some valuable insight on the debate, the majority of his arguments are unsubstantiated and oversimplified, and reveal his clear bias.

To begin, Redd presents that "America's future is at stake." Before he has even begun to present the arguments, Redd presents readers with a logical quandary. Here, Redd attempts to use pathos to draw readers in and refocus the issue on education's greater effect on the nation and not its costs. However, he gives us no evidence to support this claim. He offers no data or backing to support his warrant. He expects readers to simply understand that and how the nation's future is inherently tied to how well education is presented and received. He compounds with "nearly everyone agrees that education is one of the biggest factors that will determine the nation's fate going forward." "Nearly everyone" is not a strong ethical claim. Is "nearly everyone" educators, politicians, policy makers or others who would have an informed opinion about the nation's fate? Even so, Redd offers no evidence to prove that the nation's future is at stake or that education is the main solution. Until readers have a definitive answer on "everyone's" credibility, they cannot be expected to make decisions based upon those opinions.

In the very next paragraph, Redd presents his bias for free college through pathos. He says the cost of higher-education leaves "many [students] ill-equipped to find good employment, let alone attain the American dream." Redd does not give us any measure of how ill-equipped students are. He uses loose terms such as "good employment" and "the American Dream." Neither have clear definitions or interpretations. One can achieve what is commonly considered "good employment" without going to college. For example, someone may choose to become a mechanic or open a restaurant. Those are two forms of gainful employment which do not require a college degree. Arguably, neither is forfeiting their claim at the American Dream. Additionally, Redd is removing focus from the issue at hand and presenting that achieving the "good life" is really what is at stake here.

  Redd continues by presenting the background on publically funded higher-education and how it became necessary for higher-education to come at the expense of the students. He adds to the credibility of the argument that something needs to be done about the monetary demand for students. He presents clear and valuable data about collegiate attendance, higher-education costs, financial aid and scholarship grants, student debt, and post-graduate employment.

  Next, Redd presents his first argument for free higher-education. He asserts that free higher-education will "benefit the entire nation" because it provides both "private and public benefit." He continues that because many of today's employers require advanced knowledge or special technical skills, a better educated workforce would "fill many of the skill gaps that prevent America's economy from growing faster." These claims are weak and unsubstantiated. Where exactly are these "skill gaps?" Are we certain these "skill gaps" are what is preventing the growth of American economy? How does Redd reconcile unemployment, especially among college graduates, if there is apparently a surplus of "skill gaps?" Furthermore, free higher-education does not immediately beget a better educated workforce. That citizens need to be better educated does not mean that college should be free. There needs to be greater data linking under-education to the cost of education.

Redd continues that more educated people would be able to fill the "good-paying jobs that often go unfulfilled." Where is the data to support this? If this is the case, why is unemployment so high? And either way he creates a false dichotomy; suggesting that more people need to be able to go to college and receive "employer-desired credentials" does not require that higher-education be free.

  Redd proceeds to call the debate, not an economic one, but a "moral and philosophical one." He uses pathos to draw readers in and excite by using words such as "reaching potential." Once again, he makes the concern that of the good of the nation and draws away from the issue at hand. However, though calling the issue a moral and philosophical one is not inherently incorrect, it is a gross over-simplification of the debate. The debate is not simply whether or not college should be free, but rather, who should pay for college. As such, the debate cannot only be considered moral and philosophical; readers must also consider the economic side.

He summarizes the arguments for free higher-education through several unsubstantiated points. He uses phrases such as "might be," and "would be able to." However, neither of these phrases are specific enough to make judgments upon. Targeting that the existing financial aid system fails does not immediately suggest that free higher-education is the answer. It only suggests that something about the current system needs to change. Either way, readers cannot cite this as a valuable point, unless readers know for certain that the system is failing. Redd does not provide us with the information or data to say that the financial aid system is failing. Redd's points about better decision-makers, focused students that can graduate on time, graduating with student loan debt, and the widening gap between wealthy and poor families, even though there is no evidence making any of these claims true, all assert that something needs to be done about college affordability, but not that free higher-education is the answer.

Redd finally attempts to consider the feasibility of free higher-education by considering both how the government could pay for public college, and providing information on where it has worked in other nations. Immediately, he fails because he cites "some economists," as having valuable and worthwhile ideas for which the government might pay for public college. However, readers cannot speak to the economists' credibility until readers know who the economists are, and their level of mastery and influence in the field. Redd continues by suggesting several means by which the government may procure the funds necessary to remove the financial demand from the students. However, none of the suggestions are as simple as he is suggesting, or likely to come in the near future.

Redd continues by offering information about other countries where tuition is free, or of relatively low cost. He cites that schools in Europe have employed tuition-free higher education. However, Redd does not give any information about these tuition-free systems other than the amount of loan debt students graduate with. Readers have no information on the relative value of the education, employment after graduation, length of studies, or if it even seems to be working well. Readers have no information on how these programs are affecting the government in these nations or taxpayers. Even if these programs are working well abroad, there is no means to know that these programs would work well in the United States considering its population, which is considerably larger than that of the European nations.

Redd cites programs in the United States that provide free tuition for college students. He cites programs such as the *Kalamazoo Promise,* which makes students who have been continuously enrolled in a Kalamazoo public school system eligible to have one hundred percent of their higher education payed for at any public university or college in Michigan. He also cites states such as Minnesota, Oregon, and Tennessee where there are already free community college programs. However, though Redd has given us examples of where free higher-education exists in the United States, he has not given us any information about the programs. He does not tell us how much the programs are affecting taxpayers or give any indication of how they might work large scale.

Next, Redd begins to present the arguments against free higher-education. Primarily, there is an issue in that his arguments for free higher education amount to nearly thirteen hundred words, where his arguments against free higher-education amount to only about six hundred.

Redd presents that the main opposition to free higher-education is because it would "simply be too expensive for the federal and state governments to maintain long-term" leading to higher taxes, and a hurt economy. This is an oversimplification of the argument. If the government is going to pay for students to attend college for free, it must be able to say where the money to do this is coming from. It is not a question of maintenance specifically, but of funding.

Redd continues to state that "Canada, South Korea, and Japan have already proven that free higher-education isn't necessary for building some of the world's most educated workforces." This is beside the point. Just because free higher-education isn't strictly necessary does not necessarily follow that it is not worth the pursuit of free-higher education. Redd also states free higher-education would not "be enough to promote the big improvements in social mobility that are needed throughout America." Once again, Redd is removing focus from the issue and putting the focus on the betterment of the nation. Even if it were a valid point, that free education by itself would not be enough does not conclude that it should not be instituted at all, or that it wouldn't be even a little beneficial.

Redd presents a few more arguments against free higher-education. Some are well thought out and defended with reasonable data. However, Redd states that "many students would still have to borrow money for their living expenses" and would not be able to leave school completely debt free. That students may not be able to leave college completely debt free does not mean that the government shouldn't try to subside at least some of the cost.

After all, isn't it valuable that students be able to graduate with only a couple thousand dollars of debt, rather than tens of thousands? Red also states that "students may not learn to be financially literate." While the concern is admirable, arguably, it's not college's job to teach students how to become mature adults. It's the parents' job. If a parent chooses to teach their own child financial literacy by having them assume the responsibility of their college payments, that is their own choice. However, college itself cannot be made responsible.

    Finally, Redd presents his arguments for the alternatives. Redd suggests a loan repayment system based upon income. Firstly, he asserts that the "problem is that this option is only available to low-income people that can prove that they are experiencing financial hardship." With this statement, he indicates a clear bias: that college should be free or as cost efficient as possible. His concern for this arrangement is not whether or not it will succeed, but that it does not succeed in the way he would like for it to. Secondly, his arguments on this point are vague. He mentions "some former college students in the US." He continues to formulate this argument through pathos, building on readers' excitement. However, he does not give any indication of which state this program is being enacted in, how well it's working, and what it is costing the local and federal government and subsequently, taxpayers.

    He also cites Australia's *Higher Education Loan Program*. He explains the program well and gives an explanation of how it is working and the effect is having on Australian government. He even gives an indication of how its shortcomings are being overcome. However, he merges into a pathos argument that this program is particularly good for artists, musicians, and writers and that the United States should take on a program like it because the world "needs" them and that "our future would be bleak without them." One cannot say for certain that the world "needs" any one person. That creates a value system whereby society decides what people are needed more than others. Couldn't one make the argument that since society also need doctors and lawyers, arguably more than society need artists and musicians, that this help should go only to aspiring doctors and lawyers? One cannot say that the future would be bleak without a certain group of people. Since it cannot be objectively rendered or calculated, readers cannot trust this point. What is the measure of bleakness? How can one say that our future wouldn't be *better* off without them?

  Redd concludes this argument saying that though taxpayers would still help fund, the "tax requirements *would likely be much lower...*" Until Redd can provide something more concrete, definitive evidence perhaps, that taxes will be lower, readers cannot take this into account when deciding upon their opinion.

  Redd argues a few more points of alternatives. Most are oversimplified in that enacting them would not directly lead to the outcome he desires, or at least would not be as simple to enact as he is presenting. In particular, Redd says individuals should discourage "the distribution of merit-based financial aid to wealthy students." If a scholarship is "merit-based," by definition, the only thing that should be considered is a student's merit, not their social status or wealth, or rather their parent's wealth.

  Redd does not present the arguments for and against free higher-education well. He presents a clear bias towards free higher-education. On both sides, he presents arguments supported by unsubstantiated evidence, over-simplified arguments, and weak analogies. He leaves us asking more questions than he answers. Redd cannot be considered a valuable source of information upon which readers may figure out upon which side of the debate they fall.

Connor Tomlin Haynes
Did Donald Stump the Nation?

 Donald J Trump: the greatest man to ever grace the face of the planet, or so some might say. President Trump might have been the most polarizing presidential candidate in this country's history, with some praising him as the anti-politician America needs and others criticizing his brash stances. He has been known as a businessman, billionaire, reality television star, and now President, a title few thought would ever come to him. And in the long tradition of Presidents before him, Trump stood before the nation and delivered an inaugural address, setting the tone for his term as commander-in-chief and accomplishing items on his own agenda. Despite any possible moral or political objections, newly elected President Donald Trump effectively used the rhetorical situation to encourage his supporters that they made the right choice in voting him into office.

 Although one might be tempted to think that President Trump was addressing the entire nation with his inaugural speech, his true target audience was his current supporters—the ones who elected him into office. Though he seemingly includes broad groups of people in many of his phrases, like "you, the people" and "everyone watching across America… this is your country," his real target audience is only composed of those who voted for him. He wants to show he will carry through with the promises of his campaign and stick up for the "little guy" who put him in power. In fact, the whole rhetorical situation is one focused on power. Trump is addressing the people who just elected him into the highest rank in the nation; not only does he feel the immense proportions of his capabilities, he wants his audience to feel empowered because he is in power. He says, "We...are now joined in a great national effort to rebuilt our country," at this very moment because he views the people who voted for him as participating in the "historic movement" for a better America by putting him in the power seat. As is seen throughout the speech, it turns out he understands his audience quite well. Those who voted for him are mostly middle-class, evangelical Caucasians or strict Republicans who voted more on the party platform—disregarding the lack of qualifications of the candidate—and are cautiously optimistic for the novelty he brings to the White House. Either way, he uses what he knows about his audience to his advantage.

In order to establish his authority, as a President who otherwise has very little in the realm of politics, Donald Trump appeals to strong religious ties present in most of his audience. Since he won 81% of the evangelical vote (Smith), Trump knows that the "almighty creator" is an authority figure to most of his audience, even if he is not. He says, "The Bible tells us how good and pleasant it is when God's people live together in unity," and continues on about how the nation must pursue solidarity even when disagreeing. Not only does this give a reason for his evangelical supporters to love him even more—by portraying himself as a God-fearing man—but he also provides another level of evidence that his audience is not the entire nation; he knows that the entire nation is not a part of the Christian faith, and yet follows the "God's people" comment with the pronoun "we," indicating his audience is indeed those who identify as Christians along side him.

President Trump maintains his portrayal as distinct from other politicians to boost his credibility with his audience, who feels scorned by the government. A popular narrative floating around the conservative rhetoric is that current politicians take the working class's hard-earned money and give it to those who do not deserve it. Trump reiterates that narrative in this very speech knowing that middle class Republicans accept that story and would appreciate a President who is the opposite of these things. Trump uses this to his advantage and reinforces the fact he is not a politician by saying things like "the establishment protected itself" and "they celebrated in our nation's capital," purposefully distancing himself from any corrupt politician who ever had power before him.

After establishing his credibility, Donald Trump focuses mainly on emotion, especially appealing to his audience's sense of patriotism. Patriotic images of the "great American flag" and "red blood of patriots" flood the far reaches of Trump's speech; these images stir the passions deep inside the cholesterol-clogged hearts of nationalists in his audience who still believe America is built on a foundation of guns, hot dogs, and sweet, sweet liberty. They have no reservations about the brazen inequalities and nastiness that have long infected the oldest roots of our country, and take Trump at face value like they have from the beginning of his campaign. Their minds are blinded by the American flag waving in their face and not only cease to care about some illogical statements the President makes, but praise Trump for standing up for traditional, American values.

Also in the realm of sentiment and passion, President Trump makes broad, absolute proclamations that the audience wants to hear, regardless of whether or not he can truly keep his promises. Some might criticize his overuse of sweeping statements, but they are perfect for his audience and their sheep-like following of Trump. If they had to do all the "thinking" when they voted for him, why would they think critically of his statements here? He makes claims about all the ways he will rebuild the nation like "the forgotten men and women of our country will be forgotten no longer" and the audience believes every word. He says this to come off as the savior of the nation, the answer to everyone's prayers. Later on he says, "I will fight for you with every breath in my body." It is significant that he struggles against these issues for the American people and not with them; he is the king who sits on the throne and fixes all the nation's problems with a wave of his hand, and those who voted for him are gratified, knowing that they played a part in Trump's charity efforts.

Although critics claim Trump has abandoned all use of logic, one can find the smallest appeals to reason sprinkled throughout his speech, which is all he needs. One particular example of a logical flow occurs when he says, "Americans want great schools for their children, safe neighborhoods for their families, and good jobs for themselves. These are just and reasonable demands of righteous people and a righteous public." Trump retains an unstated premise in this quote that the American people are a righteous public—which all people want to wholeheartedly believe about themselves—and the audience agrees. Just using the word "reasonable" appeals to his audience's sense of logic. Many might say he was not logical enough in his speech, but he understands his audience has long forgotten the days when logic was at the forefront of political stances, and therefore uses other appeals far more often.

One does not have to be a raving fan of our new President to admit he is not a dumb man. He knows it is nearly impossible to sway his opponents—after saying so many things the media deemed as outrageous—so forgets about the opposition entirely and focuses on those who already pledged allegiance to him at the polls. He said what they wanted to hear, employing every word to hit their ears just right. One might venture to say Trump is already preparing the public for his reelection but there are too many factors in the current political climate to be certain of future plans just from this speech. It is evident however that he sees himself in the victory seat and, for the moment, enjoying the spoils of winning.

References

Smith, Gregory A., and Jessica Martines, "How the faithful voted: A preliminary 2016 analysis." Pew Research Center, 9 November 2016. Accessed 16 February 2017.

Trump, Donald J. 2017 Presidential Inauguration, 20 January 2017, The White House, Washington DC. Inaugural Address.

Lila Pattison

Lila Pattison is a freshman nursing major who was raised in Oregon. Growing up as a book lover, writing became a way for her to express herself throughout her life. When she is not studying, she loves cuddling up with a hot cup of tea and a good book, as well as spending time with friends and listening to good music.

Paperman: A New Light to Lost Love

What would happen if the one that got away… really didn't get away? What if love at first sight existed and changed lives? What if those who we have the brief and yet strong connection with ended up being our soulmate? The short film *Paperman* addresses this romantic concept in a new and thought provoking way; by combing a compelling story with groundbreaking technology. It won Best Short Film at the Academy Awards, Best Animated Short Subject at the Annie Awards, and Best Animated Film at the CinEuphoria Awards; as well as being nominated for Best Animated Character for both the main characters at CinEuphoria. *Paperman* tells the story of a young businessman, George, who is locked into the drudgery of daily life as a single office-worker. As he proceeds with his normal morning routine, he runs into a young lady, Meg, and is tragically torn away from her as she continues on to an interview. The rest of the short film follows his life as he tries to get back to her, and along with the help of a fleet of paper airplanes he eventually is reunited with his long lost (or should we say hours-lost) love.

History and Formation

Paperman broke through barriers in the film world by combining the old-fashioned art of 2D sketch animation and the modern detailed craft of Computer Generated (CG) animation. Not only does *Paperman* combine them in a skillful way, but also in a way that you don't even notice the difference as you're initially watching the film; it draws you into the storyline as a means of building a new form of reality. The mastermind behind *Paperman* is a man named John Kahrs; he was animation supervisor for *Tangled*, as well as an animator in the films *Ratatouille, Monsters Inc.,* and *The Incredibles*. Kahrs states in an interview with GoSeeTalk that the questions he wanted to address in the film were; "…what if two people were perfect for each other who made

> that random connection on a street or train platform, and what if they lost each other, how would they find their way back to each other again? And maybe how would the fates conspire to bring them together if they really tried hard enough"1 (Exclusive: Interview…).

Kahrs uses Paperman to present a new and unique thought process on life and love at first sight, encouraging the viewers to not overlook the little things that happen in life, but rather to take notice of what could be mundane and find the beauty in the unexpected.

Animation Techniques

By Kahrs bringing together 2D sketch and CG animation, he is providing a background supportive argument for his main point. 2D sketch is seen as the old familiar romance, something we all can relate to and it represents the classic love story. CG brings in the new and thought-provoking perspective, complimenting the old and shining a different and unique light on the subject. By using this unique and subtle representation in the specifics of the animation in Paperman, Kahrs is subtly and tactfully adding another layer to the thought-provoking aspects of this short film.

Lighting

As a strictly black and white film, with the exception of lipstick, Paperman relies on shading and brightness to portray emotions and feeling as the film progresses. The primary means of shading come out strongly in the portrayal of sunlight and shadow; which turns out to be drastically dynamic in the setting of the city.
Sunlight

Sunlight provides not only the feeling of hope and brightness in Paperman, it represents the expectation and reality of love. Throughout the film, it forms paths and illuminates the bright spots of life as the lovers go through their daily lives on the path of fate towards their meeting again. In the following picture, the sunlight is illuminating the very alley in which all of the airplanes George has sent in Meg's direction have landed. These airplanes then form a fleet and set off in pursuit of George and Meg in a desperate, and successful, attempt to reunite the lovers. The sunlight specifically lights a path down to the fleet of airplanes, illuminating them as a last ray of hope and piquing the curiosity of the viewer.

Shadow

Shadow plays an important role in Paperman; portraying not only sadness and domination, but also a lack of freedom. Not only is darkness used in the office George works to give a sense of imprisonment, but it is also used as a portrayal of the character of people. We see George wearing a darker grey suit, bound by droll duty; dominated strongly George's boss (pictured in the following screenshot) who is wearing a black suit which portrays him as a taskmaster. Shadow strongly contrasts light, bringing in a different perspective on the monotony and drollness of everyday life; which is shaped and formed by the different shades of emotion and personalities, some of which are darker than others.

Camera Perspective

The perspective the camera takes plays an essential role in interacting with the viewer and pulling them into the story. By taking unique viewpoints, the viewer is not only drawn into the story, but also is pulled into the emotions, helping them to relate to the characters on a personal level. One brilliant example of this would be when his last airplane is taken from his hands by the wind and whisked out over the street. We watch this from over his shoulder as he desperately tries to reach out and retrieve it. It gives a sense of desperation, which we all can relate to on one level or another.

Scene Transitions

In *Paperman*, the transitions between scenes are sharp and abrupt, keeping the attention of the viewer as the story progresses. It keeps things interesting, and also gives off the feelings of desperation and anxiousness that comes with having a new love. The viewer can easily relate to the feelings of infatuation and adrenaline that comes along with the shock of the abrupt scene changes; this expresses how sudden life can feel as you first experience new love. It also stays true to the old style that the 2D animation brings to this film.

Color

One unique aspect of *Paperman* is the lack of color except for Meg's red lips, bringing a unique side to the story. The constant black and white in the film speaks so loudly of the mundane, and then Meg's lips come as an expected shock. They bring in an aspect of passion in a passionless world, and they give a spark to George's life in a way he never expected. By bringing in a new color, and that of passion, Kahrs plays with intrigue and mystery; making *Paperman* more than just a child's story. He makes it a story that an audience of all ages can relate to, and brings in an aspect of maturity.

Sharpness of Lines

One huge factor of *Paperman* that provides an underlying and subtle form of communication is the sharpness of the lines used. In the world of Paperman, lines are used to suggest not only stability and security, but also imprisonment and being locked into life. In the opening and closing scenes that show a distant shot of the train station, the sharp and bold lines under the train station provide a feeling of new security and support in his life. People naturally form a life of stability as they settle into a daily routine, as seen by the dark and enclosing buildings; and yet what humans sometimes need is to be shaken out of their monotony. Meg brings that awakening to George in Paperman, and as the film continues we see him defying the standard steadiness of life and forming a new kind of security in his life; one that is built around Meg.

Closing Thoughts

By combining 2D and CG animation, John Kahrs was able to create a masterpiece the like of which has never been seen before. Kahrs played with shading and lighting, as well as the high detail of CG and original feel of 2D animations, and managed to produce a short film that not only tells a story without words but also brings the audience into a thought provoking viewpoint on love at first sight. Rejecting the social norms that imprison us, Kahrs brings a thought process to light that rejects those ideals and presents a new take on life.

Works Cited

"Exclusive: Interview...Disney Animator & 'Paperman' Director John Kahrs." GoSeeTalkcom. N.p., n.d. Web. 07 Oct. 2016.

Kimberly Powell

To be Free or not to be Free...
That is the Question

"Feel the Bern!" crowds cheered as the elderly, white-haired man took to the podium. "Education should be a right," he vehemently declared, "not a privilege. We need a revolution in the way that the United States funds higher education" (Sanders, 2016). Students rallied and applauded on the footsteps of the U.S. Capitol as the call for free education for all rang through the air. Although Bernie Sanders's campaign ended in the primary election, the desire for change remained. Because of the increasing costs of postsecondary, many who have potential and desire to further their education find themselves unable because of a lack of funds. Others take out student loans but struggle to repay the debt. In Luke Redd's article from trade-schools.net entitled Should College Be Free? Pros, Cons, and Alternatives, he fleshes out each perspective, both for and against the idea of free education, while offering possible solutions to this growing problem in America.

    After briefly describing the obstacle of high tuition costs that many students face, Redd invites readers to harken back to the foundations of our country, to the words of John Adams: "The whole people must take upon themselves the education of the whole people and must be willing to bear the expense of it" (Redd, 2016). Later, the Morrill Act was passed in 1862 with the goal of opening up the option of higher education to lower-income individuals. Back in the early days of America, a college education was tuition-free, but over time, funding from the states has decreased as tuition costs have steadily increased, reaching rates that are unaffordable to many low-income families. Those who do attend inevitably face the burden of student debt. Analyzing statistics from the Federal Reserve, Redd discerned that "in 2015, the total amount of student loan debt in America was estimated to be about $1.3 trillion," which proved to be a dramatic increase from previous years (Redd, 2016). Yes, financial aid and Pell Grants provide some assistance on the journey through higher education, but the percentage of coverage has decreased over the years. Despite the financial roadblocks, the number of students attending college has continuously risen over the past 15 years. The U.S. Department of Education has found that "over 20 million students were enrolled in American post-secondary schools in the fall of 2015, which was almost five million more than in 2000" (Redd, 2016).

    With a basic understanding of the problem that has evolved over the years, Redd begins to explain the support for having free college for all. Economically speaking, individuals with skills obtained through a college education would better fill the open positions in today's labor force, boosting the economy in multiple aspects. Besides this measurable benefit of free college, there is also a moral standard that we as Americans must cling to. Redd believes America has always sought for equality between its citizen, and the area of education is no exception. Everyone, including those in a lower class, should have the same opportunity to enjoy the benefits of a college education. Like Bernie Sanders, some Americans view a college education as a right rather than a privilege. In order to pay for the schooling of an entire nation, Redd offers several options. An increase in taxes for the wealthiest Americans, a decrease in inefficient spending, and several other adjustments could help make this idea of free college a reality (Redd, 2016).

The concept of free tuition is not merely an American dream; in fact, several countries, particularly in Europe, have offered free college for quite some time now. Because the tuition is free, students graduate college with significantly less debt than those who graduate in American schools. Comparatively, the United States does not spend more on education than countries that do offer free education. "The U.S. spends about 1.36 percent [of the national GDP] on post-secondary education," Redd states, "But Finland, Norway, and Germany only spend 2.08 percent, 1.96 percent, and 1.35 percent" (Redd, 2016). Redd believes that if free college is a reality in other countries, then America should be no exception. Some states have already begun to offer free community college, while others are in the process of passing laws to create two-year programs that are of no cost to its students. Kalamazoo, Michigan has been one of the most proactive leaders in the pursuit of free public education. As a result of the Kalamazoo Promise, students from low-income homes have a higher chance of choosing to go to college to better their future.

As one can imagine, there exists a detailed opposition to having free college education in America, particularly among the upper class. Taxes, for instance, would dramatically increase, having a harmful effect on the households and the economy at large. Additionally, making college free, Redd explains, would not necessarily solve the problem. Many students are simply unable to learn in those particular environments and would not succeed given the opportunity. And many who do take the chance still do not succeed. Redd states that "only about 20 percent of first-time, full-time students at public two-year colleges earn associate's degrees, diplomas, or certificates within three years of starting" (Redd, 2016). And furthermore, since free-college would only be offered to public schools, those who would fair better in a private school might not be able to afford education without the support from financial aid. Ultimately, students may become less motivated because they no longer have to worry about funds, which would increase dependency on government and decrease the value of hard work.

Redd offers an alternative to the previously mentioned options, a method that remains affordable without fearing a high increase in taxes. Instead of the constant rates that newly grads must pay off, he suggests a system where individuals pay back debts based on their income levels. In this system, there should be no interest attached to the loan itself, and because college is not altogether free, taxpayers would not suffer as much. Unlike a free-college system, this alternative route holds the students responsible for their actions while in college, increasing the personal value of hard work and dedication. Despite the long list of alternatives, the author leaves the ultimate decision up to the reader. It is the reader who determines which stance to choose, but furthermore, it is the reader alone who determines which stance to choose, but furthermore, it is the reader alone who can determine the validity of Redd's argument. Although he is able to thoroughly explain both sides of the argument as well as the alternatives, the author commits several logical fallacies, which ultimately detract from his overall ethos as a writer and makes his argument less effective.

Before diving into the argument presented, it is necessary to evaluate the author's credentials; however, when viewers of the website go to look for the website's author, they will come up empty handed, for there is no reference to the author on the website itself. Upon entering the URL into an automated bibliography maker, the name Luke Redd appeared. After further investigation on the web, his Google + profile proved to be the only source of reliable information in regards to his background. According to his profile, Redd does not have any expertise or education that would make him a credible source of information. His profile merely states that he "writes about education, careers, and life" and works for the website Trade-Schools.

This website, as many websites do, contributes a bias that prevents valid arguments from being discussed over the course of Redd's article. Trade-Schools goal, as described on its homepage, is to provide options for career training, opening eyes of potential students to the many schooling options. Additionally, the website offers tools to locate nearby schools. Because the website has a heavy focus on pursuing additional education after high school, Redd's essay does not leave mention alternatives to post-secondary. In many of his arguments, he relays the idea that people will not succeed or be happy in life without getting a college degree of some kind. In his opening paragraph, Redd states the following:

> When the cost of attending college, university, or trade school is too high, a lot of students simply choose not to pursue a higher education. And that leaves many of them ill-equipped to find good employment, let alone attain the American dream (Redd, 2016).

Because the bias of the website seeks to promote further education, the possibility of succeeding without an education does not exist. Despite Redd's attempts to provide a well-balanced argument for free education, he ignores many alternative possibilities due to a hasty generalization.

His hasty generalization is but one of many logical fallacies that Redd commits throughout the course of his article, the first of which is found in his opening argument for free education. In the midst of a bullet point list of reasons in support of the idea, Redd states, "People would have more freedom to contribute their talents...which could lead to happier people. And happier people could lead to a happier, more prosperous nation as whole" (Redd, 2016). While this may seem to be a logical conclusion, Redd's reasoning does not provide enough evidence for the conclusion drawn. This slippery slope fallacy is indicative of either a poorly researched topic or a lazy writer.

In hopes of making up for his own lack of credibility, the author commits another logical fallacy, one that appeals to higher authority. When questioning whether free public college was a viable option in America, Redd asserts in the opening paragraph that certainly the heads of America believe so. "You don't have to look any further than President Obama. Free [community] college...is something that he has proposed" (Redd, 2016). Although his reference is relatable to readers, Redd fails to adequately support his claim partly because he does not provide further detailed information on the topic but also because Redd is relying too heavily on the credibility of the President rather than his own ethos.

Furthermore, as if both of these fallacies were not serious enough, the author, either out of ignorance or intentionality, misinterprets some references, picking out information that supports his argument rather than accurately describing the context itself. When attempting to establish a precedence for free college early in his article, Redd stated, "The Morrill Act of 1862 enabled land-grant colleges to be created by states so that higher education could become available to Americans of every social class" (Redd, 2016). Although affordability has resulted from the enactment of the Morrill Act of 1862, it was not originally created for that purpose. According the Encyclopædia Britannica, the act was meant to establish colleges focused on "agriculture and mechanic arts" as opposed to the many liberal arts colleges available at the time (Land-Grant College Act of 1862, 2017). Redd, in hopes of supporting his viewpoint, mistakes the results of the act for what original intention of the act actually was. He claimed that the purpose of the act was to offer a college education to those in lower social classes when in reality the purpose of the act was to merely establish certain types of colleges.

Later, he discusses multiple examples of tuition free college in other countries, raving about how students in countries such as Denmark, Estonia, and Germany graduate with significantly less debt than those in the United States (Redd, 2016). Additionally, Redd highlights how these other countries do not spend significantly more on education than the United States currently does, so having free college would not be a major burden on the government. What Redd fails to acknowledge is the many downsides to free education in those other countries. According to the Organization of Economic Co-operation and Development, these countries have drastically higher taxes than the United States has currently (Jackson, 2015). The burden of tuition falls on the people as a whole rather than entirely the individuals attending college, which may seem nice, but defeats the purpose of making life more affordable. Furthermore, the percentage of students enrolled in college is much lower in these other countries than in the United States (Jackson, 2015). Since there are fewer individuals attending college in these other countries, it is consequently less expensive to foot the bill for college education. Redd's article highlights only the favorable aspects of free education in other countries that support his argument, failing to acknowledge the negative parts.

Because of the length of Redd's article, one would think that each perspective is thorough and well thought out, yet the opposite proves to be true. With a closer look at the details of the article, the reader finds several claims that seem powerful but lack backing or any sort of explanation. After briefly describing the historical background of free college, Redd bullet points random facts and statistics but provides no backing or explanations for the claims. In his later uses of bullet points, Redd takes the liberty to express various hypothetical situations while supplying no factual information for support. When discussing the reasons for free college, Redd states, "Many of America's top-performing high school students never apply to the most challenging colleges and universities even though they have the ability to succeed in them" (Redd, 2016). However, he never takes the time to support this statement with factual information such as a statistic or expert testimony. His lack of explanation in various circumstances not only leaves the reader with several unanswered questions but also damages his ethos in an unsalvageable manner.

To be free or not to be free. That is the question that remains unanswered upon reading the conclusion of Redd's article; however, when questions arise concerning the effectiveness of the article itself, they are answered with a long list of fallacies committed in various ways by a cursory author. Luke Redd's lack of expertise in combination with the website's bias set a weak basis for his seemingly thorough argument. Because of his hasty generalizations, misinterpretations, and lack of explanation, Redd's article proved to be much less effective than it could potentially have been.

References

Jackson, A. (2015, June 25). 'Free' college in Europe isn't really free. Retrieved February 27, 2017, from http://www.businessinsider.com/how-do-european-countries-afford-free-college-2015-6

Land-Grant College Act of 1862. (2017, January 18). Retrieved February 27, 2017, from https://www.britannica.com/topic/Land-Grant-College-Act-of-1862

Redd, L. (2016, March 4.). Should College Be Free? Pros, Cons, and Alternatives. Retrieved February 21, 2017, from http://www.trade-schools.net/articles/should-college-be-free.asp

Sanders Calls for Student Loan Reforms, Affordable Tuition. (2016). Retrieved February 21, 2017, from https://www.sanders.senate.gov/newsroom/press-releases/sanders-calls-for-student-loan-reforms-affordable-tuition

Expository

Tristan Galyon
Kelsey Howell
Johnna Willis

Tristan Galyon

Turbocharging

It seems that everything is getting the word "turbo" attached to it these days; "turbo" has become a sort of buzzword to denote something fast, whether it be modern electronics such as the Droid Turbo, or even tax software such as Intuit's TurboTax. In the context of automobiles, many ordinary passenger cars have a "turbo" version or trim level. This "turbo" indicates an engine equipped with a turbocharger, which is often sportier and more luxurious. Almost everyone must own and regularly drive a car at some point in their lifetime; some see cars as something to be enjoyed, and others see them as an appliance to be used simply as transportation. Regardless, turbocharging improves a car's ability to fulfill either requirement; it increases both fuel economy and performance. This essay explores the technology of turbocharging and its increasing presence in the automotive industry.

In order to understand turbocharging, a technology designed to increase an engine's performance, it is helpful to understand exactly how a car's engine works. A turbocharger works to increase the amount of air and fuel in an engine, which generates more power and does so in a more efficient manner. A car engine is an internal combustion engine, meaning it combusts a mixture of fuel and air to generate power and subsequent rotational energy to spin a car's wheels. A turbocharger improves this by increasing the amount of air (and subsequently, the amount of fuel) per engine cycle, in turn providing both an increase in power and an increase in fuel efficiency, which improves the experience for nearly all drivers. In detail, a car engine operates on "engine cycles", which are made up of four "strokes". Each stroke is one movement of the piston, which is connected to the crankshaft via a connecting rod. The piston moves up and down, and it rotates the crankshaft with each cycle; this transition to rotational movement is what enables a car to spin its wheels.

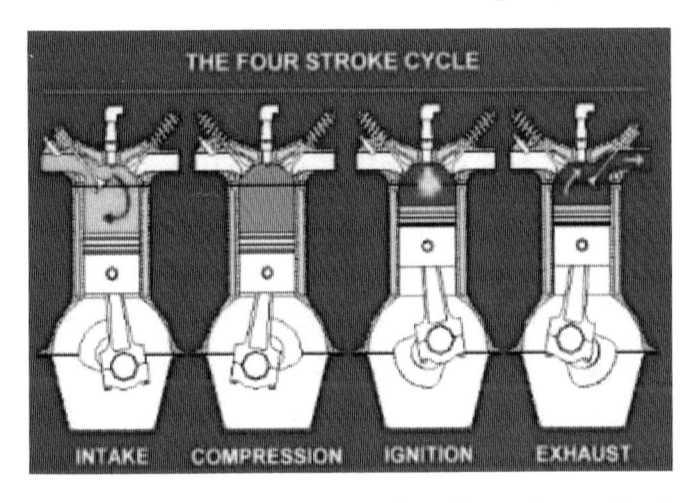

THE FOUR STROKE CYCLE

INTAKE   COMPRESSION   IGNITION   EXHAUST

The first part of an engine cycle is the intake stroke, in which the piston is moving down, drawing air into the cylinder via a valve at the top. At the same time, fuel is injected into the same combustion chamber, formed by the sides of the cylinder and the top of the piston. After that is the compression stroke, during which the valve is closed and the piston moves up, compressing the air/fuel mixture. When the piston reaches the top of the cylinder, the air and fuel are ignited by the spark plug during the ignition stroke. The force of this combustion forces the piston down, causing the crankshaft to rotate; as it rotates, the then-rising piston forces all of the spent exhaust gases out of the engine through an exhaust valve at the top of the cylinder. In all of these steps, air plays a critical role. Dr. Evangelos G. Giakoumis is a professor of mechanical engineering and oversees the internal combustion engine laboratory at the National Technical University of Athens. Succinctly, he says of gasoline engines: "it is the incoming air-supply that plays the most critical role for the engine response." (Giakoumis 2016). Without air to compress, the engine would simply be lighting gasoline on fire, which creates no combustion and thus no energy.

A turbocharger works to bring more air into the cylinder. According to BorgWarner, a major turbocharger manufacturer, "In exhaust gas turbocharging, some of the exhaust gas energy, which would normally be wasted, is used to drive a turbine... which draws in the combustion air, compresses it, and then supplies it to the engine." (BorgWarner, n.d.). Dr. Jianqin Fu of Hunan University in Changsha, China conducts research at the Research Center for Advanced Powertrain Technology, and he describes the process in more detail: "Because the IC engine exhaust gas has a high temperature and high pressure (compared with ambient pressure), it still contains lots of energy which could be recovered by exhaust turbine. In the exhaust turbocharging system, exhaust gas is used as the working medium of turbine, while turbine acts as the power output device of boosting pressure system. During the exhaust gas expansion process, part of exhaust gas energy is recovered and transformed into useful work. Then, the useful work is used to drive the compressor". (Fu et al. 2014).

The turbocharger acts as an intermediate step between exhaust and intake; the exhaust gas, which is normally routed out of the engine and through pipes out of the back of the car, is routed through the turbocharger. This turbocharger acts as a compressor, using the exhaust gases to spin a turbine that compresses the new air coming into the engine during the intake stroke. Since the air going inside the engine is already compressed, "the oxygen molecules are packed closer together. This increase in air means that more fuel can be added for the same size naturally aspirated engine." (Cummins, 2016). Dr. Giakoumis, the aforementioned professor of mechanical engineering and internal combustion engine expert, says of exhaust gas turbocharging: "By so doing, the air-supply that enters the cylinders is increased accordingly, enabling efficient burning of proportionately higher amount of fuel. The obvious benefit here is the direct increase in the engine power; at the same time, down-sizing of the engine is possible" (Giakoumis 2016). Below is a graphic showing air routing through an engine and turbocharger system, as well as specific air routing through the turbocharger itself.

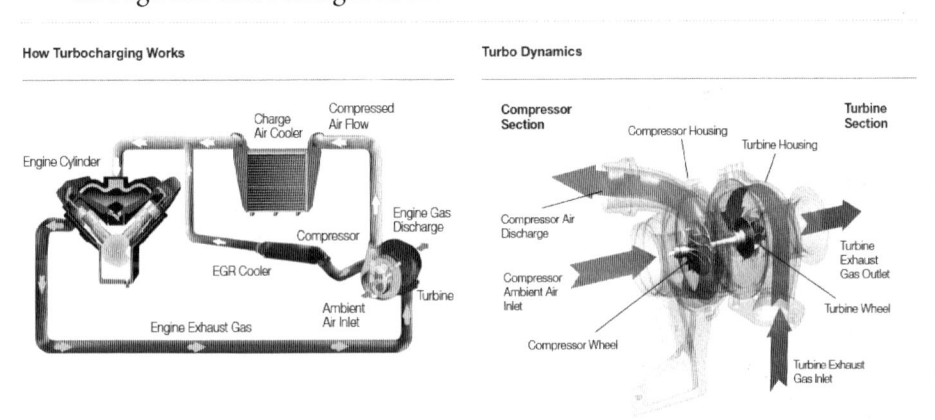

How Turbocharging Works

Turbo Dynamics

Turbocharging improves engine performance by increasing efficiency, which impacts one's life more than is immediately apparent; with both an increase in power and an increase in fuel efficiency, the experience is improved for nearly all drivers. More efficient engine operation results in improved fuel economy and reduced emissions, and improved engine operation can lead to other benefits. "[Turbocharging] generates increased mechanical power and overall efficiency improvement of the combustion process. Therefore, the engine size can be reduced for a turbocharged engine leading to better packaging, weight saving benefits and overall improved fuel economy." (Cummins, 2016).

Jason Cammisa, an automotive journalist for *Road & Track*, a leading auto magazine, said, "[Turbochargers] are the right way to reduce emissions without sacrificing performance." [Cammisa 2015]. On the other end of the spectrum, high performance vehicles are often turbocharged in order to achieve high amounts of horsepower and torque. Rather than using the increased energy efficiency of a turbocharger to decrease engine size and minimize the amount of fuel used, high-performance turbocharged engines use the extra air and fuel provided by a turbocharger to further increase the power generated by an engine already tuned for high performance applications. The cars produce more horsepower, and more torque generated at a lower RPM, meaning that the power is easier to access for the driver; a turbocharged engine makes more power, sooner. Cammisa also says of supercar brand Ferrari: "Modern Ferraris do what you ask, when you ask, how you ask. They are pretty much perfect... their forthcoming turbocharged replacements will almost certainly be faster." (Cammisa 2015). In the sense of power generation and performance, an exhaust gas turbocharged engine "has many advantages, such as higher specific power, smaller displacement, and larger torque. As a result, [exhaust gas turbocharging] has been widely applied in automotive gasoline engines in recent years," (Tang et al. 2016). In the sense that large amounts of horsepower and torque are benchmarks for high-performance engines, turbochargers help achieve that goal. Additionally, they do so without disregarding secondary goals, such as limiting emissions and fuel consumption. Oftentimes, initiatives to heighten performance sacrifice nearly all other goals in order to maximize power output. These conventional methods of making power are single-faceted; they lack the ability to contribute to multiple goals of an engine. Giakoumis says, "A distinctive advantage of a turbocharged engine is its capability to operate more efficiently compared to its naturally aspirated counterpart, hence, produces proportionately less CO2 " (Giakoumis 2016). Though Giakoumis specifically talks about carbon emissions, he makes the point that reduced emissions stems from more efficient engine operation. More efficient operation means less fuel consumption, less oil use, and less carbon and soot particle emissions.

Turbocharging increases the energy efficiency of an engine by using exhaust gas, an energy source that is nearly free. Exhaust gas, without a turbocharger equipped, would leave the exhaust pipe at the rear and be effectively wasted. Harnessing the exhaust gas energy through the use of a turbocharger is harnessing an incredible previously untapped power source. The exhaust gas is very hot and moves relatively fast; it "contains a lot of thermal energy, thus exhaust gas energy recovery becomes an effective way to improve engine fuel efficiency and power performances." (Tang, et al. 2016). To Dr. Fu, "exhaust turbocharging engine has more advantages, e.g., higher thermal efficiency, for the compressor power comes from exhaust gas energy recovery becomes an effective way to improve engine fuel efficiency and power performances." (Tang, et al. 2016). To Dr. Fu, "exhaust turbocharging engine has more advantages, e.g., higher thermal efficiency, for the compressor power comes from exhaust gas energy rather than IC engine," (Fu, et al. 2014). Fu's differentiation of the compressor's power source as being the exhaust gas is important because he explicitly highlights the effectiveness of using that free energy source to improve efficiency.

The rising presence of turbocharged engines in the automotive industry indicates a shift towards more efficient methods to increase both fuel economy and performance. Since a car's engine is an internal combustion engine, it combusts a mixture of fuel and air to generate power and subsequent rotational energy; a turbocharger allows for larger amounts of both, and in turn for more efficient engine operation. Efficiency in operation is pertinent not only to issues of fuel consumption and emissions, but also to issues of performance. Nearly everyone drives a car, and a turbocharger has such an impact on the behavior of a vehicle that it directly impacts the experience the driver has with the car. The application of a turbocharger is one that contributes to both of these goals; it doesn't neglect one in favor of the other. With regard to the constraining of emissions and the maximizing of both fuel economy and horsepower/torque, automakers are consistently turning towards turbochargers with great success.

Bibliography

BorgWarner Turbo Systems. (n.d.). Principles of Turbocharging. Retrieved March 20, 2017, from http://www.turbos.bwauto.com/products/turbochargerPrinciples.aspx

Cummins Turbo Technologies. (2016). How a Turbocharger Works. Retrieved March 20, 2017, from http://www.cumminsturbotechnologies.com/our_technologies/how_a_turbocharger_works

Fu, J., Liu, J., Wang, Y., Deng, B., Yang, Y., Feng, R., & Yang, J. (2014). A comparative study on various turbocharging approaches based on IC engine exhaust gas energy recovery. Applied Energy, 113, 248-257. doi:10.1016/j.apenergy.2013.07.023

Giakoumis, E. G. (2016). Review of Some Methods for Improving Transient Response in Automotive Diesel Engines through VariousTurbocharging Configurations. Frontiers in Mechanical Engineering, 2. doi:10.3389/fmech.2016.00004

Honeywell Turbo Technologies. (n.d.). Turbo Fundamentals | Honeywell Turbo Technologies. Retrieved March 20, 2017, from https://turbo.honeywell.com/turbo-basics/turbo-fundamentals/

Tang, Q., Fu, J., Liu, J., Boulet, B., Tan, L., & Zhao, Z. (2016). Comparison and analysis of the effects of various improved turbocharging approaches on gasoline engine transient performances. Applied Thermal Engineering, 93, 797-812. doi:10.1016/j.applther-maleng.2015.09.063

Kelsey Howell

Kelsey Howell is a freshman athletic training major from Tanzania and China. She enjoys reading books, especially historical fiction. Soccer is her favorite sport to play and when she is not playing sports she is spending time with friends in the great outdoors.

Proprioceptive Neuromuscular Facilitation

According to Dr. Phil Page from *The International Journal of Sports Physical Therapy*, "human movement is dependent on the amount of range of motion available in synovial joints" (110). The amount of tension in the surrounding muscles can limit the range of motion in synovial joints (Page 110). In order to release tension and allow full range of motion, many individuals, especially athletes, stretch the muscles that are tight. There are a few main methods of stretching: dynamic stretching, static stretching, and proprioceptive neuromuscular facilitation (PNF). People in many different settings are familiar with dynamic and static stretching, whereas few outside the clinical setting understand PNF stretching. PNF is a specific kind of stretching that "involves a shortening contraction of the opposing muscle to place the target muscle on stretch, followed by an isometric contraction of the target muscle" (Victoria 623). There are two major PNF techniques, both of which are effective due to the specific physiological mechanisms of autogenic and reciprocal inhibition that they utilize. PNF is similar in many ways to the popular method of static stretching, but differs significantly from the popular stretching method called dynamic stretching.

When athletic trainers speak about PNF, they use a specific set of vocabulary to describe what is taking place inside the body.

The first set of terms that athletic trainers use are the ones that refer to the stretching method itself: *proprioceptive, neuromuscular,* and *facilitation.* According to Irvin, the word *proprioceptive* "means receiving stimulation within the tissues of the body" (149). He describes this technique as a *proprioceptive* technique because it utilizes the nerves involved with *proprioception,* which is the "awareness of posture and movement" (570). *Neuromuscular* is the term that athletic trainers use because the technique involves both the nervous system and the muscular system (Irvin 149). And finally, *facilitation* means the "promotion or hastening of a natural process" (Irvin 149). Therefore, proprioceptive neuromuscular facilitation is a process that uses the interaction between the proprioceptive nerves and the muscles that they control in order to hasten the natural healing process. The next set of terms that athletic trainers use are the terms isotonic and isometric. These two terms describe types of muscle contractions. An isometric contraction is a muscle contraction where the muscle length stays the same throughout the contraction, and an isotonic contraction is a muscle contraction where the muscle length changes through the contraction. Finally, one more set of terms that athletic trainers use are the terms agonist and antagonist. The agonist muscle refers to the muscle that the athletic trainer is stretching. The antagonist muscle refers to the muscle that works counter to the agonist muscle. When the agonist muscle contracts, the antagonist elongates, and when the antagonist contracts, the agonist elongates.

There are two major PNF techniques that athletic trainers use for stretching. The first and most common technique is the contract-relax technique. In this technique, the athletic trainer assisting the patient being stretched will passively place "the restricted muscle into a position of stretch" (Victoria 624). The athletic trainer will then give a verbal command for the patient to push, and the patient will contract the agonist muscle. The contraction can either be an isometric or an isotonic contraction based upon the athletic trainer's goal for the PNF session. If the athletic trainer's goal is to stretch out the tight muscle, then he or she will use an isometric contraction. The patient holds the isometric contraction for a at least three seconds at "20%-50% of [the patient's] maximal effort" (Victoria 624). If the athletic trainer's goal is to rehabilitate an injury, then he or she will use an isotonic contraction. The patient contracts muscle groups through a pattern of movement while the athletic trainer provides resistance to those movements (Surburg and Schrader 36).

The second major PNF technique is the contract-relax-contract technique. This technique is similar to the contract-relax technique, except it takes the stretch one step further. The patient performs an isometric contraction with the agonist muscle against the resistance that the athletic trainer provides. Once the patient releases the contraction, he or she will contract the antagonist muscle against resistance that the athletic trainer provides for the same amount of time and at the same level of effort (Victoria 625).

Both of the major PNF techniques are effective because they utilize a physiological mechanism called autogenic inhibition. Autogenic inhibition is a reflex "that occur[s] when the Golgi Tendon Organs (GTOs) in the tendons of the [target muscle]…detect harmful stimuli" (Briggs 107). The Golgi Tendon Organ (GTO) is a sensory nerve that is embedded into the muscle fibers. When it detects possible injury to the muscle by over-extension, it sends a message to the brain that tells it to tighten up the muscle. However, if "a sustained contraction has been applied to the [GTO] for longer than 6 seconds," then the GTO relaxes and the muscle elongates (Victoria 627). Therefore, the athletic trainer gives the verbal command to contract the agonistic muscle. If the patient is able to contract the agonist muscle against the resistance that the athletic trainer provides for at least six seconds, then the GTO will give the signal to release and relax, giving the patient the ability to stretch the agonist muscle farther (Briggs 107).

 The contract-relax-contract method makes use of another physiological mechanism called reciprocal inhibition. Reciprocal inhibition is based on "the way in which the [agonist] muscle and its antagonist muscles work together" (Briggs 107). In the final contraction of the contract-relax-contract method, the patient will contract his or her antagonist muscle against resistance provided by the athletic trainer. When the antagonist muscle contracts, the agonist muscle elongates to help allow for the contraction of the antagonist muscle (Briggs 107). By adding this additional way of elongating the agonist muscle, the contract-relax-contract PNF technique attempts to increase the chances of the agonist muscle being elongated by utilizing multiple physiological mechanisms.

 The common type of stretching that PNF is most similar to is static stretching. Static stretching, according to Dr. Page, is a "traditional…type [of stretching]…where a specific position is held with the muscle on tension to a point of a stretching sensation and repeated" (110). What makes static stretching different than PNF is that static stretching does not involve any muscle contraction to facilitate muscle elongation. They both are similar, however, in the fact that according to a study by Jerome Danoff, "static and PNF stretching…[do] not significantly change power performance" (1532). Both of the methods of stretching engage the muscle in continuous tension "beyond the normal range of motion," which engages the mechanism of autogenic inhibition (Danoff 1532).

Danoff theorizes that static and PNF stretching "may produce inhibition that diminishes the number of available motor units, thereby limiting force and power output" (1532). Because static and PNF stretching limit the force and power output, neither stretching technique is effective for increasing the power performance of the muscle (Danoff 1532). However, both PNF stretching and static stretching effectively increase range of motion (Page 112).

Dynamic stretching is another common form of stretching that many are familiar with, however it has many differences with PNF stretching. Instead of holding a muscle contraction for a short period of time, dynamic stretching involves "moving a limb through its full range of motion to the end ranges and repeating several times" (Page 110). Dynamic stretching involves not just one target muscle like PNF and static stretching, but often is a routine that "incorporate[s] continuous and rhythmic movements" which target muscle groups that are specifically related to the particular activity that the individual is about to engage in (Danoff 1528). Danoff found in his study that dynamic stretching increased "power for both slow and fast movements," particularly when compared to the change in power after static and PNF stretching (1531). As a result, dynamic stretching is a popular technique to engage in pre-exercise, "especially among competitive athletes" because it is more effective at enhancing muscular performance (1531).

Proprioceptive neuromuscular facilitation stretching is a unique form of stretching that uses the body's physiological mechanisms to help increase range of motion. The two major techniques, contract-relax and contract-relax-contract are effective due to their use of the physiological mechanisms of autogenic and reciprocal inhibition. PNF stretching and static stretching are comparatively similar, however dynamic stretching and PNF stretching are considerable dissimilar forms of stretching. Even though it may not be the most well-known method of stretching, PNF can be an effective method of increasing range of motion.

Works Cited

Brigss, Wyatt, et. al. "Proprioceptive Neuromuscular Facilitation (PNF): Its Mechanisms and Effects on Range of Motion and Muscular Function." Journal of Human Kinetics, vol 31, 2012, pp. 105-113.
National Center for Biotechnology Information, ncbi.nlm.nih.gov/pmc/articles/PMC3588663/.

Danoff, Jerome, et. al. "Acute Effects of Static, Dynamic, and Proprioceptive Neuromuscular Facilitation Stretching on Muscle Power in Women." Journal of Strength and Conditioning Research, vol. 22, no. 5, 2008, pp. 1528-1534.

Irvin, Richard, et. al. Glossary. Sports Medicine. 2nd ed., Prentice Hall, 1998, 567-571.- - - "The Warm Up Period and Athletic Conditioning". Sports Medicine. 2nd ed., Prentice Hall 1998, pp. 26-39.

Page, Phil. "Current Concepts in Muscle Stretching for Exercise and Rehabilitation." The International Journal of Sports Physical Therapy, vol. 7, no. 1, 2012, pp. 109-119. National Center for Biotechnology Information, ncbi.nlm.nih.gov/pmc/articles/PMC3273886/.

Surberg, Paul, and John Schrader. "Proprioceptive Neuromuscular Facilitation Techniques in Sports Medicine." Journal of Athletic Training, vol. 32, no. 1, 1997, pp. 34-39. National Center for Biotechnol ogy Information, ncbi.nlm.nih.gov/pmc/articles/PMC1319233/.

Victoria, Gidu Diana, et. al. "The PNF (Proprioceptive Neuromuscular Facilitation) Stretching Technique - A Brief Overview." Science, Movement and Health, vol. 13, no. 2, 2013, pp. 623-628.

Johnna Willis
A Homeschool Survey

    Parents in America possess freedoms in way they choose to raise their child. One of these freedoms is the opportunity to choose how their child is educated. Today, the three main options for education are government or public schools, private schools, or homeschooling. In the past thirty years, the number of families choosing to homeschool has increased dramatically. The parents' option to homeschool has changed throughout history, but today in the United States children are homeschooled in a variety of ways for several reasons. Factors influencing the homeschooling system in America today include the history of home education, the motivation to pull children out of public school, and the states' variations homeschool opportunities.

    The history of home education in America goes back to the birth of the nation but has developed over time. Homeschooling has been an option for centuries but has only been prevalent in America for a few decades. Joseph Murphy says in his book *Homeschooling in America* that homeschooling was the primary source of education before there were public schools. Therefore, many of the founders of our country were homeschooled. However, once public schools established across the country, homeschooling became less popular. The public educational system took about seventy years within the nineteenth and twentieth centuries to spread state to state. Homeschooling then seemed "old-fashioned" and less normal. It didn't take off again until the late 1900's when complaints were made about the public-school system (Murphy, 2014, p 31).

Many think homeschooling became popular once again as the result of conservative parents keeping their children out of the public-school system. However, *Homeschool: An American History* says otherwise. "In the 1960s most conservative efforts were aimed at keeping public school values consistent with their own" (Gaither, pg 107). Instead of pulling their kids out of school, conservative families were attempting to change the schools they already attended. Years passed by and the schools wouldn't typically change to the standards parents desired for their children. Many parents believed although the schools could provide their children with adequate education, the parents or tutors at home could provide excellent education and a better environment. This began the slow rise of homeschooling numbers in America until it reached the 1.77 million children recorded in 2012 (*Homeschool Statistics*, 2016).

The parents of those 1.77 million children had issues with public school other than just if the education was adequate. The National Standards of Education Statistics (NSES) program conducted a study in the 2011-2012 school year asking parents why they decided to homeschool. The most common answer was a quarter of the parents told the NSES that they were concerned about the environment at the local schools, 19% felt like the academics would be more appropriate for their child (or children) if the parents chose the materials, 16% said they wanted to homeschool due to religious reasons, and 40% gave a variety of other reasons such as special needs and frequent relocation (*Statistics About Nonpublic Education in the United States*, 2015).

Liza Rivero talks about this issue as well. In her chapter *Reasons for Homeschooling* she answers the question "Why homeschool?" with, "Because it allows children to learn at their own pace... it provides a safe learning environment... it strengthens and nurtures families... [and] because all children's needs are worthy of special attention" (Rivero, 37-41) and based on the NSES program, this is a solid answer.

These reasons might be plenty enough for some states to accept a parent's decision to homeschool. Some states require even less. Mitchell Stevens, who has done extensive research on homeschooling and reports most of it in his book *Kingdom of Children*, found a difference in the reports state by state. "Home education is legal throughout the United States, but states vary widely in the extent to which they require homeschool parents and their children to report to educational authorities" (Stevens, pg 13).

The Home School Legal Defense Association (HSLDA) mapped out the states that are the easiest and most difficult in which families can homeschool. Regulations vary by region. High regulation states (5 states, all in New England) are required to turn in to the state the student's test scores, teacher certification, house tests, and get their curriculum approved by the state. Moderate level regulation (19 states nationwide, including Hawaii) requires turning in to the state the student's test scores. Low regulation states (15 states, mostly in the south and the west) just requires informing the state of the student no longer attending local schools. Some states (11 states nationwide, including Alaska) have no regulations (*Homeschool Statistics*, 2016)

Throughout these demographics homeschooling regulations aren't the only things that vary. Every state offers different opportunities to homeschoolers. Parents who choose to educate their children at home also have various opinions as to how they want to homeschool. Some of these education forms are solely at home with different curriculum and some involve meeting in groups or meeting in a virtual classroom.

One popular form of education used in homeschool settings is classical education. Many private schools nationwide also offer classical education programs due to the focus on the trivium. The trivium consists of three stages of learning: the grammar stage (elementary), the dialectic or logic stage (junior high), and the rhetorical or speaking stage (high school).

Lisa Rivero speaks about her knowledge of classical education in *The Homeschooling Option*, "The three stages of learning—the trivium—do seem to follow many children's intellectual development. When used with flexibility and adaptation for the individual child, classical homeschooling is a good fit for many families and students, and it offers a reassuring educational plan and structure that sets the tone for lifelong learning" (Rivero, p 86).

Though classical subjects may be popular, another form of homeschooling follows the same pattern and curriculum as a public school. Some parents check and see what their child would be doing if they were in public school and educate them with the same books. This can be difficult, but it has been done.

Other parents do not want to use the same books as a public school, but they do want the children to be working on the same curriculum as others their age with teachers. Nationwide there are groups of homeschoolers who meet in "cooperation groups" or "co-op." These groups typically consist of several homeschool families in a region. "Co-op" groups can go on field trips together, have book clubs, have PE classes, and other specialty classes. The bulk of work is done at home by each individual family, but once or twice a week the children can interact with classmates in these regular homeschool groups.

Another form of homeschool that is rapidly expanding is online education. Online education programs can be full enrollment or by the subject. Some programs are on the computer but not using internet such as disc-based programs. Hybrid courses have self-taught and digital materials, but other courses are fully online. Public schools across the country also have systems that can be accessed online with government funding (*Online Elementary School Glossary*, 2016).

Online education probably didn't occur as a future option for children when the Founding Fathers discussed education for America's children, but they also probably never realized how large the public schools would become after two hundred years. The change in home education in the past century has made it a reasonable option for families today. These changes, along with reasons to homeschool and the government's variety of homeschooling methods, are some of the main reasons why homeschooling has become so popular today. Children around America spend days walking the hallways of "co-op" groups and houses rather than with several hundred other students in the local public school. This number of students today, influenced greatly by the past, will also be students who change the world for the future.

Resources

Davis, T. (2013, September). *The Most Home-School-Friendly States in the US (and the least)*. She Knows. Retrieved October 15, 2016, from http://www.sheknows.com/parenting/articles/1018417/which-states-are-best-for-homeschooling

Gaither, M. (2008). *Homeschool: An American History.* New York, NY: Palgrave Macmillan.

Homeschool Statistics. (2016). Retrieved October 14, 2016, from https://www.time4learning.com/homeschool/homeschoolstatistics.shtml

Miller, C. (2003, April). On the Trivium. Retrieved October 20, 2016, from http://www.classical-homeschooling.org/trivium.html#learn

Murphy, J. (2014). *Homeschooling in America: Capturing and Assessing the Movement.* New York, NY: SkyHorse

Online Elementary School Glossary. (2016). Retrieved October 20, 2016, from http://www.accreditedschoolsonline.org/k-12/online-elementary-school/

Rivero, L. (2008). *The Homeschooling Option: How to Decide When It's Right for Your Family.* New York, NY: Palgrave Macmillan.

Statistics About Nonpublic Education in the United States. (2015, June 9). Retrieved October 16, 2016, from http://www2.ed.gov/about/offices/list/oii/nonpublic/statistics.html

Stevens, M. L. (2003). *Kingdom of Children: Culture and Controversy in the Homeschooling Movement.* Princeton, NJ: Princeton University Press.

Argument

Kelsey Howell
Brandon Ryan

Kelsey Howell

The Proper Use of Proprioceptive Neuromuscular Facilitation

With the current emphasis on sports performance and the availability of improved research and medical technology have come many advancements in the area of sports medicine and performance enhancement. One area where this is increasingly apparent is in the variety of methods of muscle stretching. The three most common techniques are dynamic stretching, static stretching, and proprioceptive neuromuscular facilitation (PNF). Dynamic stretching involves "moving a limb through its full range of motion to the end ranges and repeating several times" (Page 110). Static stretching, on the other hand, involves holding a stretched position "for 20 to 30 seconds" (Reynolds). PNF stretching is "promoting or hastening the response of the neuromuscular mechanisms through stimulation of the proprioceptors and other sensory potentials of the sport participant" (Irvin 149). Athletes use these three methods of stretching as both rehabilitation methods and pre-event stretches. While all three are effective at increasing range of motion, some are more ideal to practice in certain situations than others. Even though it can be an effective method of increasing range of motion as a pre-event stretch, athletes and sports medicine professionals should limit the use of proprioceptive neuromuscular facilitation to therapeutic settings because dynamic stretching is more effective than PNF at maintaining muscle power and performance as a pre-event stretch for athletes, and PNF is a highly effective method of rehabilitation.

Dynamic stretching is a more effective stretch than PNF at maintaining muscle power and performance as a pre-event stretch. The reasoning behind this assertion is dependent on two facts. First, many studies show that dynamic stretching does not sacrifice muscle power and performance for range of motion in the same way that static stretching does. Second, the mechanics and effects of static stretching are similar to those of PNF. If dynamic stretching is more effective as a pre-event stretch than static stretching, and static stretching and PNF stretching are similar, then it follows that dynamic stretching is more effective as a pre-event stretch than PNF.

Many researchers have conducted studies that prove that dynamic stretching is more effective at maintaining muscle power and performance than static stretching is. Thomas Little from Staffordshire University and Alun Williams from Manchester Metropolitan University conducted a study in 2006 on the "effects of differential stretching protocols during warm-ups on high-speech motor capacities in professional soccer players" (203). They had professional soccer players conduct 3 different warm up routines within a week, each more than 48 hours apart (203). The first routine involved static stretching in addition to warm up exercises in order to increase heart rate and blood flow. The second routine involved dynamic stretches in addition to warm up exercises, and the third involved no stretching at all and relied solely on exercises to increase heart rate and blood flow (Little 204). After completing the warm up protocol for the day, the players participated in various performance tests. Little and Williams tested the players with a vertical jump, a 10-meter sprint, a 20-meter sprint, and an agility course. Little and Williams designed the performance tests to assess "leg power, acceleration, maximal speed, and agility capacities" (204). The results of the study indicated that every player obtained the best results on all the tests, save the vertical jump, after participating in dynamic stretching (Little 205). They particularly noted that "there were significant differences among the warm-up protocols for agility, with dynamic stretching resulting in significantly better performance than static stretching and no stretching" (205). Because of the superior performance of the dynamic stretching as opposed to the static stretching, Little and Williams recommend that sports requiring high-speed performances utilize dynamic stretching as part of the pre-competition warm-up (205-206).

Mohammadtaghi Amiri-Khorasani from the Shahid Bahonar University of Kerman conducted a similar study in 2016 on the way that different stretching methods included in pre-event warm-ups affect the acceleration and speed of soccer players (179). He had 20 collegiate soccer players randomly divide into five groups, and each group performed a different warm-up protocol on non-consecutive days (Amiri-Khorasani 180). The first of the various warm-up protocols involved no stretching, the second involved dynamic stretching followed by static stretching, the third involved static stretching followed by dynamic stretching, the fourth involved dynamic stretching, and the final protocol involved static stretching (Amiri-Khorasani 182). After the warm-up protocol each group tested their acceleration performance by running a 10-meter sprint and a 20-meter sprint (Amiri-Khorasani 180). Amiri-Khorasani's results back up the results of Little's and William's study, proving once again that dynamic stretching is more effective than static stretching. Amiri-Khorasani states, "the current findings show that DS [dynamic stretching] during a warm-up is more effective than SS [static stretching] as a preparation to the abrupt acceleration and speed required in soccer" (185). M. P. McHugh and C. H. Cosgrave of the Nicholas Institute of Sports Medicine and Athletic Trauma authored a review of various studies on the roles of stretching in injury prevention and performance, which also showed that dynamic stretching is more effective than static stretching. McHugh and Cosgrave noted that "it is clear that an acute bout of stretching will decrease the ability to generate a maximal force" (179). Based on the evidence of the research many have put forth on the subject, it is clear that dynamic stretching is "better suited for athletes requiring running or jumping performance" (Page 114).

However, some will argue that while dynamic stretching is better at maintaining muscle power and performance, that does not mean that it is a more effective pre-event stretch. McHugh and Cosgrave concluded in their review that the majority of the studies show "that pre-participation stretching in addition to a formal warm-up [does] not affect injury risk compared with a control group performing a warm-up without stretching" (176). Contrary to the majority of the findings however, they do discuss some studies that show positive results of static stretching on injury risk. McHugh and Cosgrave reference a study conducted on thigh strains in military recruits where there was a 1.2% prevalence of muscle strains in the control group but only 0.3% prevalence in the stretching group (176). McHugh and Cosgrave also reference another study done on military recruits where stretching "resulted in a 67% reduction in muscle strains and low back muscle injuries combined" (177). While there is some evidence that static stretching pre-event may help reduce muscle strains in particular, "further research is needed in this area" in order to draw any firm conclusions (Cosgrave 179).

Static stretching and PNF are similar forms of pre-event stretching; therefore, dynamic stretching is also better at maintaining muscular power and performance then PNF stretching is. Dr. Phil Page, certified athletic trainer and physical therapist in Baton Rouge, Louisiana states that "several studies show similar increases in ROM and performance when comparing pre-contraction stretching (PNF) and static stretching" (114). It is also evident from the studies that both PNF and static stretching decrease strength (Page 114). Meaghan Maddigan and her colleagues performed a study comparing various PNF techniques with static stretching. She concluded that the PNF techniques and static stretching both "provided similar improvements in the ROM [range of motion] and poststretching performance decrements in MT [movement time]" (abstract). Based on the evidence that both static stretching and PNF result in similar decreases, and 3.4% decrease in the athletes' movement time with both stretching techniques, she makes the recommendation that "athletes should not use these techniques before important competitions or training because of the impairment of … MT" (abstract). If both static stretching and PNF stretching result in similar decreases in muscle performance, and dynamic stretching is more effective at maintaining muscle power and performance as a pre-event stretch than static stretching is, then it follows that dynamic stretching is a more effective pre-event stretch than PNF stretching.

Some researchers, on the other hand, have provided evidence that suggests that PNF and static stretching may not in fact yield similar results. Dr. Page touches on the controversy in his commentary "Current Concepts in Muscle Stretching for Exercise and Rehabilitation". He states that "some authors report that both static and pre-contraction stretching are able to increase acute hamstring flexibility, which others suggest static stretching of PNF stretching are more effective" (Page 114). Wyatt Briggs and his colleagues at Willamette University reference a study on the way stretching affects the hamstring and gastrocnemius (calf) muscles (110). Static stretching, dynamic stretching, and a PNF stretching technique were the three stretching methods that the study focuses on. The subjects participated in the stretching methods three times a week and their range of motion was measured before the treatment, after 11 rounds of treatment, and after 21 rounds of treatment (Briggs 110). Surprisingly, the results indicated that "the longer the treatment time, the less significant the results differed among the three treatments" (Briggs 110). Another study that Briggs references in his article on PNF evaluated various stretching methods, and he summarized the conclusion of the study by stating that "significant increases in ROM [range of motion] were seen throughout the treatment groups, but it was found that the PNF techniques were more effective than the SS [static stretching] method for both hip flexion and shoulder extension" (111). The results of this study point to the fact that it is possible that while PNF and static stretching are similar, they do not yield exactly the same results. Therefore, some can conclude to claim that because static stretching is less effective at maintaining muscle power and performance than dynamic stretching, PNF stretching is also less effective than dynamic stretching, would be an illogical conclusion. PNF is in fact not similar to static stretching, but is able to yield superior results in some areas. Researchers must conduct more studies comparing PNF and dynamic stretching directly before making the assertion that dynamic stretching is more effective at maintaining muscle power and performance than PNF stretching.

Not only is there research that proves that dynamic stretching is more effective at maintaining muscle power and performance as a pre-event stretch than PNF, but there is evidence showing the significant effectiveness of PNF as a therapeutic methodology. Briggs mentions seven studies that researchers conducted on the effects of PNF and summarizes the conclusion that all seven studies came to: "The results of these seven studies discussing ROM [range of motion] imply that PNF… increases ROM and flexibility in all of the subjects (111)." One of the studies that he mentions targeted four muscle groups: the gastrocnemius, the ankle dorsiflexors, the hip adductors, and the hamstrings. The researchers treated each of those specific muscles with a PNF technique except for the ankle dorsiflexors (Briggs 110). The researchers treated the ankle dorsiflexors with the ballistic stretching method, which is a form of dynamic stretching that involves "'bouncing' at end range of motion" (Page 110). After 14 rounds of treatment the group treating the ankle dorsiflexors switched to the PNF method because "flexibility was increased more with the [PNF] method than with the [ballistic stretching] method" (Briggs 110). The PNF technique ended up being the most effective method of stretching in the rehabilitation process. In comparing the effectiveness of static stretching and PNF stretching as methods of therapy, Dr. Page states that "patients with knee osteoarthritis can benefit from static stretching to increase knee ROM; however, PNF stretching may be more effective" (115). Dr. Page also observes that "athletes with hamstring strains recover faster by performing more intensive stretching than by performing less intensive stretching" (115). PNF is a more intense form of stretching than static stretching because it involves continuously desensitizing the nerves that protect the body's muscles from stretching too far. Stretching, then contracting, followed by more stretching has more of an intense effect on the stretching reflex than simply static stretching does.

PNF is not merely a highly effective method of therapy, but was in fact developed for the very purpose of aiding "the rehabilitation of clients with spasticity and weakness by facilitating muscle elongation" (Victoria 623). A physical therapist named Margaret Knott and a doctor named Herman Kabat designed PNF specifically for the rehabilitation of "neurological dysfunctions" (Victoria 623). It was obvious early on that the new rehabilitation method the experts developed and called PNF was effective. Because the new rehabilitation technique was so successful, physiotherapists and others involved in health and sports medicine began to explore additional application for the new method of therapy (Victoria 623). The technique has "broad applications in treating people with neurologic and musculoskeletal conditions," therefore it is a useful tool in the rehabilitation of many musculoskeletal injuries (Victoria 623). Recently, PNF techniques "have been used as a stretching technique for increasing flexibility" in place of or in addition to other methods such as static stretching and dynamic stretching (Prentice 110). However, it may function less than ideally outside of the therapeutic uses for which Knott and Kabat developed it. If Knott and Kabatt designed it initially for the purpose of therapy, and it functions extremely well in that capacity while functioning less ideally in other applications of the technique, then it follows that PNF use should be limited to therapeutic settings.

However, some will argue that PNF is not always the best method to use in therapy. Dr. Page observes that while it was designed for neurological dysfunctions, it does not have a positive effect all the time. He mentions a specific situation where this is the case, stating that "stretching appears to have no benefit for neurological patients who have had a stroke or spinal injury" (Page 115). Not only that, but others will also argue that while PNF causes a decrease in muscle power and performance in high intensity activities, PNF is in fact an effective method to increase performance in low intensity performances. Briggs states in his article on PNF and its mechanisms and effects that "although PNF may decrease performance in high intensity exercises, it has been found to improve performance in submaximal exercises such as jogging" (109-110). If PNF stretching can be effective to improve performance in low intensity exercises, then athletes should still be able to utilize PNF as a pre-event stretch before low intensity performances instead of limiting it to simply therapeutic settings.

    More pressure is put on athletes on a regular basis to get any edge to compete, and some have turned to new methods of stretching to help give them that extra advantage over their opponent. Margaret Knott and Dr. Herman Kabat originally developed PNF as a method of therapy for neurological problems, however its application is widening to assist in various aspects of athletic performance and enhancement. PNF does increase range of motion, but it also decreases muscle power and performance. Dynamic stretching, on the other hand, is able to increase range of motion to a functional range for the athletic activity while increasing muscle power and performance. Because there are other methods of pre-event stretching that not only assist with increasing functional range of motion for that athletic activity, but also increase muscle power and performance, sports medicine professionals should not consider PNF as a viable method of pre-event stretching. They should limit its use to the therapeutic setting which Kabat and Knott designed it to be effective in. By limiting the use of PNF to therapeutic settings and utilizing dynamic stretching as a pre-event stretch, the athlete will be able to maintain maximum muscle power and performance, and therefore will be able to perform at the highest level possible.

Works Cited

Amiri-Khorsani, Mohammadtaghi, et. al. "Acute Effect of Different Combined Stretching Methods on Acceleration and Speed in Soccer Players." Journal of Human Kinectics, vol. 50, 2016, pp. 179-186. 10.1515/hukin-2015-0154

Brigss, Wyatt, et. al. "Proprioceptive Neuromuscular Facilitation (PNF): Its Mechanisms and Effects on Range of Motion and Muscular Function." Journal of Human Kinetics, vol 31, 2012, pp. 105-113. National Center for Biotechnology Information, ncbi.nlm.nih.gov/pmc/articles/PMC3588663/.

Irvin, Richard, et. al. "Rehabilitation Following Injury." Sports Medicine. 2nd ed., Prentice Hall 1998, pp. 137-157.

Little, Thomas and Alun Williams. "Effects of Differential Stretching Protocols During Warm-Ups on High-Speed Motor Capacities in Professional Soccer Players." Journal of Stretching and Conditioning Research, vol. 20, no. 1, 2006, pp. 203-207.

Maddigan, Meaghan. "A Comparison of Assisted and Unassisted Proprioceptive Neuromuscular Facilitation Techniques and Static Stretching [Abstract]." Journal of Stretching and Conditioning Research, vol. 26, no. 5, 2012, pp. 1238-1244. The Journal of Stretching and Conditioning Research, 10.1519/JSC.0b013e3182510611

McHugh, M. P. and C. H. Cosgrave. "To Stretch or Not to Stretch: The Role of Stretching in Injury Prevention and Performance." Scandinavian Journal of Medicine and Science in Sports, vol. 20, 2010, pp. 169-181. 10.1111/j.1600-0838.2009.01058.x

Reynolds, Gretchen. "Stretching: The Truth." The New York Times. The New York Times, 31 Oct. 2008, www.nytimes.com/2008/11/02/sports/playmagazine/112pe warm.html?_r=1&ref=health. Accessed 15 Nov. 2016.

Page, Phil. "Current Concepts in Muscle Stretching for Exercise and Rehabilitation." The International Journal of Sports Physical Therapy, vol. 7, no. 1, 2012, pp. 109-119. National Center for Biotechnology Information, ncbi.nlm.nih.gov/pmc/articles/PMC3273886/.

Prentice, William E. "Conditioning Techniques". Principles of Athletic Training: A Competency Based Approach. 14th ed., McGraw-Hill 2011, pp. 82-121.

Victoria, Gidu Diana, et. al. "The PNF (Proprioceptive Neuromuscular Facilitation) Stretching Technique - A Brief Overview." Science, Movement and Health, vol. 13, no. 2, 2013, pp. 623-628.

Brandon Ryan

Brandon Ryan is a nursing major at Cedarville University. He comes from Michigan where he enjoys going to Lake Michigan and basking in the sun. He loves hearing jokes, playing piano, competing in sports, and wrecking in video games. One of his wishes is that denim overalls will come back into style in his 20s.

Pom Beanies are the Best

    Most people tend to view winter's icy chill as the most horrid of feelings. In response, they adhere to the saying, "comfort over style" and never hesitate to inquire of themselves a question: why not have both? It almost seems an obvious question for anyone to ask. If one wants to look good and also feel good, should people deny them their rights? A person's standards should not have to be lowered so that they can pretend everything is fine in the worst of the worst conditions. Style should be promoted through - if not made priority over- comfort, specifically on the head. A pom beanie achieves style, comfort, and convenience, and because of this, it should be worn by anyone who has a head.

    The style of a beanie turns heads and can change an average joe into an above average joe. Fashion artists always pressure the people to clomp around in their noisy shoes and wear tight, layered clothes that weigh them down with the desire to make a good impression. Granted, they may look more professional, but that is not a look someone strives to have all day and all night. People desire the look of a relaxed, chic, and amiable soul. Think of the dads who always try to be "hip" when their child's friends come over, but sagging pants, no-sleeves, and sideways hats are no match against the pom beanie. The pom beanie's smooth style shows everyone who's the wisest in the trends. People never wish for a stress-filled, occupational look in their lives, but rather, they are excited for the casual work days or the times they can wear sweatpants. This stress-free look for a body is also available for the head in the form of a pom beanie which radiates to the world a sense of tranquility when one cozily places this soft piece of clothing around their ears. The image of peace is a picture that people have always wanted, and the pom beanie is sure to deliver this with each glamourous thread giving satisfying a glowing warmth.

For those crazy people who desire more than style in their clothes, the pom beanie also delivers comfort for their head. There is a reason that a person with the luck of wearing a pom beanie appears to be in a distant, blissful paradise. It is because they *are* in a blissful paradise, though not so distant. Only the Pom Beanie can form an oven to bake the bread inside while acting as a wreath of puppy fur (no puppies are harmed in making beanies, unless they go blind from staring at the pom beanie's blinding glory, but that can't be helped). It gives a feeling of contentment that is only increased with the addition of sweatpants and a sweatshirt. Just imagine sweatpants, in all their warm satisfaction for the legs, as a hat. The pom beanie is the secret ingredient to the chef's masterpiece, the wife to the husband, the candy to the kid, the crutch to the guy shouting, "Give me back my crutch!" It is not needed in life, but it sure makes everything a billion times better. Winter's brutal flanks can no longer break the lines of thread surrounding the precious fort nor will the form-fitting walls be breached by cloud catapults firing precipitation at the skulls below. Everything annoying, ranging from pesky mosquitos searching for their next victim to the subarctic water dripping down from the roof, will soon taste defeat as the wearer feels continuous victory with the ultimate defender up top. It is surprising that these pieces of clothing are not prescribed by every doctor who has had a basic education as they increase happiness and comfort which in turn betters one's health. Literally, emotionally, spiritually, metaphorically, soliloquy, and analytically, there is no downside to the pom beanie. No other headpiece can erase the feeling of discomfort and emptiness on the bare head like the pom beanie, the protector from strong winds, and the defender from freezing temperatures.

    In addition to achieving both style and comfort, the pom beanie also rewardingly remains a convenient piece of headwear usable anytime and anywhere. No place is the wrong place for a pom beanie. Outside? Wear it. Inside? Go ahead. In the dorm? Perfect! In the shower? Sure! Why not? The tool to happiness is acceptable in all places because one should be happy everywhere. Moreover, pom beanies work just as well as night caps as they do day caps since they complement the bed in making one feel cozy and look good while sleeping. The comfy head translates into a comfy bed for true beauty sleep. Then in the morning, a person will awake with that same, lasting comfort continuing through the rest of the day. Truly, any time is the perfect time to wear a pom beanie since it is an accepted piece of expression and coziness. Class time becomes an hour to learn *and* relax. Dinner time is no longer a satisfaction to the stomach but also to the head. The enjoyable moments spent with friends can be made that much more fantastic now that a piece of light, magical material is available for the deprived head. The number of inconvenient times to wear this miracle fabric is about as minimal as the number of juveniles on the nice list. The few months of summertime might cause the hat to be a little too overwhelming, but the pom beanie would still be a refuge of comfort inside the air-conditioned home. The boundaries that contain the reasonable moments to wear a pom beanie are almost endless.

As an owner of one of these fine hats, I am privileged to pick up and slip on my helmet of luxury. As I bask in the luxurious ocean of comfort, I am riddled with all sorts of accusations and questions. Some say that they can achieve this same level of comfort with a regular beanie, but there is no reason to look like a swimmer so to have a warm head. People dare to ask what the difference between a pom beanie and pom-pom beanie is. It seems obvious that there are two poms instead of one, which is just too much and too absurd since one pom is lighter and just as successful at its task. Those skeptics also state that the pom beanie can only be worn with a few outfits. Nonsense! The pom beanie looks fresh with every get-up. Worn with tuxedos, khakis, dresses, jeans, suits, pajamas, or shorts, the pom beanie always creates that chill and snug vibe. To other people, all that was previously stated is not enough to make them wear this hat. Seriously, can't they be content with what they are already given? If all of this is not enough and there needs to be a more "life-bettering" reason other than the ones previously stated, a reason that will leave all of the pom beanie's competitors in the dust, then here is one. Many products claim to be the most satisfying, and they use a crazy argument to push their claim, but the pom beanie doesn't need to do such things. The pom beanie doesn't need to because it is undoubtedly the best and will surely help in anyone's pursuit of glory and riches.

There really is no negative side to the pom beanie save maybe for one thing. Anything as awesome as the hat and the wearer of it will find themselves surrounded by haters. Haters who claim that their bare heads can stand the discomfort that life throws at them, who think a pound of hair gel and a comb will outdo the magnificent piece of tapestry in hat form, who, in the end, are only jealous of the paradise that rests on a different head than their own. People will chuckle at an "absurd" piece of clothing but then turn their faces away in jealousy, carefully controlling the temptation to snatch the crown off the majesty's cranium. The pom beanie conveys the image of tranquility desired by all and equally serves to comfort a person's most valuable part of their body which is why this style and comfort should be presented anywhere that one brings his head. It really is a gateway to a convenient experience filled with comfort that also advocates style which is why I urge everyone to share in this life-changing clothing.

  This essay has its high points and low points. A high point of my essay, I believe, was the humor. I felt I wasn't forcing it too much, except in a few parts, but I always kept a happy, joking tone. I am proud of the comparisons made between the pom beanie and a king's crown in the concluding paragraph (pg. 4), and I enjoyed making the hypocritical statement at the end of the first paragraph also on page four. I am also really glad that overall I still kept a clear structure even though I was also focusing on the hyperbolic descriptions.

  One of the low points included an unintended, sexist statement. In my conclusion paragraph, I had stated that men would be struggling to keep their girls focused on them. This statement assumes that women only look for the best-looking man and will not stay loyal to their man if he is not current with the trends. It also assumed that only men wear pom beanies. I looked to the "sexist and biased language" section in our handbook, which explained to "avoid occupational or social stereotypes" (pg. 168).

Even though the whole essay was meant to be silly, after careful examination, and the fact that the sentence was also a little confusing, I decided to take it out entirely.

Notes

Composition Student Learning Outcomes

By the end of first year composition, students will:
- Apply knowledge of conventions through proper formatting, documenting, and structuring of written text, controlling such surface features as syntax, grammar, punctuation and spelling.
- Use technology to locate and evaluate information as well as produce their own writing
- complete each stage of the writing process toward producing a cohesive text
- respond appropriately to various rhetorical situations
- apply critical researching, reading, and writing skills in order to integrate their own ideas with those of others
- display a biblical worldview through written or oral coursework

Grading System

A – Recognizes excellent achievement. It is indicative of superior quality work and reveals a thorough mastery of the subject matter. The student receiving this grade should demonstrate enough interest to do some independent investigation beyond the actual course requirements.

B – Indicates work and achievement that are well above average. The student receiving this grade should be capable of doing advanced work in this field. The quality of the work should be considered better than that achieved by the average student.

C – Indicates average achievement and a satisfactory meeting of requirements.

D – Reveals inferior accomplishment and is generally unsatisfactory from the standpoint of course requirements.

F – Failing grade. It indicates very unsatisfactory work. No course credit is earned.

Plagiarism: What It is and How to Recognize and Avoid It

What is Plagiarism and Why is it Important?

In college courses, we are continually engaged with other people's ideas: we read them in texts, hear them in lecture, discuss them in class, and incorporate them into our own writing. As a result, it is very important that we give credit where it is due. Plagiarism is using others' ideas and words without clearly acknowledging the source of that information.

How Can Students Avoid Plagiarism?

- To avoid plagiarism, you must give credit whenever you use
- Another person's idea, opinion, or theory;
- Any facts, statistics, graphs, drawings—any pieces of information—that are not common knowledge;
- Quotations of another person's actual spoken or written words; or paraphrase of another person's spoken or written words.

These guidelines are taken from the Code of Student Rights, Responsibilities, and Conduct.

Cedarville University Writing Center

Director: Professor Isaac Mayeux Digital Communication Center Room 104 Cedarville University

Phone: 937-766-3245

Email: The Writing Center

Mission: The Cedarville University Writing Center exists to help writers at all levels of proficiency from all academic disciplines develop effective writing skills. This development takes place primarily through one-on-one peer consultations which are adapted to individual writers' needs. Such consultations will be competent and timely, will occur in a comfortable, non-threatening atmosphere, and will address all writing projects in any stage of the writing process, from brainstorming to revision. These consultations focus primarily on the writing at hand, but the long-term goal for every session is to help each tutee become a better writer overall. The center is neither a proofreading service nor a classroom- tutors do not edit or grade. Instead, the center blends service and communication, a blend which at its core is wholly Christian.

Centennial Library

Department Contact Numbers

- Administration: 937-766-7845
- Circulation Desk: 937-766-7840
- Collection Services: 937-766-7844
- Curriculum Materials Center: 937-766-7854
- MediaPLEX: 937-766-7852
- Reference Desk: 937-766-7850 • Office FAX: 937-766-2337
- Public FAX: 937-766-3776

Hours

- Monday - Thursday: 7:45 am - 11:30 pm
- Friday: 7:45 am - 7:00 pm
- Saturday: 10:00 am - 7:00 pm
- Sunday: 7:30 pm - 11:30 pm